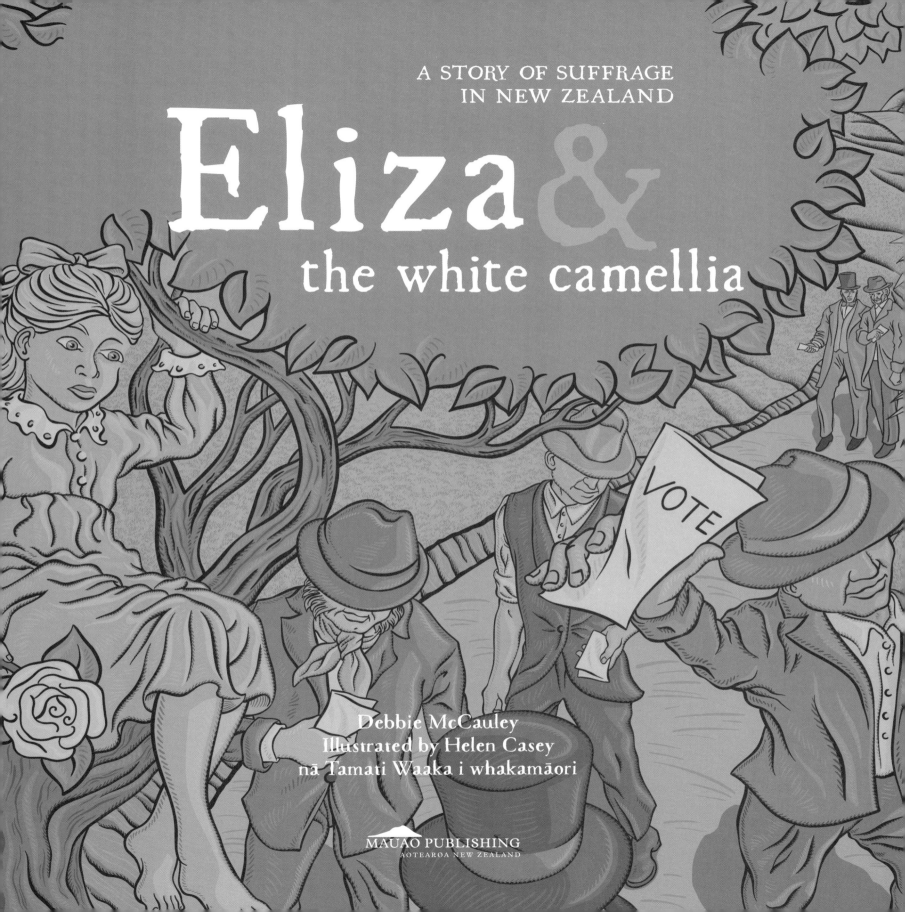

A STORY OF SUFFRAGE
IN NEW ZEALAND

Eliza&
the white camellia

Debbie McCauley
Illustrated by Helen Casey
nā Tamati Waaka i whakamāori

MAUAO PUBLISHING
AOTEAROA NEW ZEALAND

DEBBIE McCAULEY is an award-winning author and publisher of several children's books. Eliza, who inspired this story, is her paternal fourth great aunt. As a feminist with a long-time appreciation of the suffragists and suffrage movement, it was fitting that in 1993 she was the recipient of a Suffrage Centennial Year Scholarship marking 100 years since New Zealand women gained the right to vote.

HELEN CASEY is a working artist, illustrator and drawing teacher with a diverse style ranging from finely detailed drawings to colourful and highly textured mixed media paintings. Helen works from the Makara Art Gallery, her own gallery on the wild and beautiful Wellington coast of Makara Beach. Here she continues to be inspired by the natural world, while her work is showcased to the public.

TAMATI WAAKA (Ngāti Pūkeko, Te Whānau ā Apanui, Tūhoe) is a native speaker of Te Reo Māori and a certified interpreter and translator with an extensive background in Māori radio, television and kapa haka. He began writing children's stories in Māori in 2007. Tamati is also involved with Te Reo Wainene o Tua, an entity that actively participates in the revival of Māori storytelling techniques.

Eliza Wallis (née Hart)

A Woman's Vote

There's a voice which calls today,
To every woman in our land,
Its thrilling accents seem to say,
'O, come, beneath our banner stand.'

Queens of our households! 'tis for you
To spread the record of our fame.
From cottage homes, and mansions too,
There breathes a power in woman's name.

Ours is a freedom, not possessed
By Britain's daughters o'er the main,
The right to vote, as we think best
For home, and conscience, not for gain.

Our mighty phalanx yet shall win,
Co-workers with our brother men,
We'll triumph over wastes of sin,
Nor cease its conflict until then.

What is our armament? Ye ask,
It is our vote, this sacred trust
Made holier, by the noble task,
Of rightly voting, when we must.

L.G. (Woodend, Canterbury, 16 October 1899).
Printed in *The White Ribbon* November 1899.

The White Ribbon was the first New Zealand
newspaper to be owned and operated solely by
women. The first issue appeared in May 1895.

Contents

> 'She is bound by the laws that men make, she has no voice in making them; she incurs her full share of all the penalties in breaking them.'
>
> Polly Plum
> *Daily Southern Cross*
> 21 February 1870

Backyards of houses in Tory Street, Wellington, 1922.

Tory Street, Wellington

Eliza Hart was likely born in Tory Street, Wellington, where she grew up. Her parents lived there for most of their lives, until their deaths in the 1880s.

Tory Street was named after the New Zealand Company ship *Tory* which sailed into Port Nicholson (Wellington Harbour) on 20 September 1839.

In 1871 the Wellington Gas Company started producing 'town gas' from coal in its Tory Street works, the first place in New Zealand to do so. This was used for street lighting, domestic lighting and cooking. Because New Zealand had a shortage of servants, women were eager to try new labour saving devices such as cookers, water-heaters, washing 'coppers', lamps, gas fires and toasters.

New Zealand's first General Election

New Zealand's first elections were held over weeks or months because of the small number of electoral officials and the difficult travel conditions throughout the country.

The 1853 election began on 14 July (Bay of Islands) and ended on 1 October (Otago), taking 2½ months to elect the 37 members of the House of Representatives, the Superintendents of the six provinces, and the 87 members of the Provincial Councils.

Parliament had to hire boats to pick up the newly elected Members of Parliament (MPs) who were due to meet for the first time in Auckland in May 1854. Canterbury MPs took 12 days to arrive via steamer, but that was nothing compared to the Otago MPs who endured a rough 10 week voyage on board a sailing ship during stormy weather. It must have been a relief when the more central Wellington became Parliament's permanent home in 1865.

First Voting in New Zealand

After the Treaty of Waitangi was signed in 1840, the British colony of New Zealand was governed from New South Wales in Australia. Self-government was granted in 1852 with the New Zealand Constitution Act. Six provinces were created: Auckland, New Plymouth, Wellington, Nelson, Canterbury and Otago. Thirteen years after the Treaty of Waitangi was signed, this Act set out the voting rules for the first General Election in 1853.

Voters had to be:

- at least 21 years old
- male
- a British subject
- have property worth £50, or to pay a yearly rental of £10 for farmland or a city house, or £5 for a rural house (Māori communal land did not qualify)
- not serving a criminal sentence for treason, a felony, or another serious offence.

VOTING PAPER.

PUBLIC MEETING.

The ELECTORS of Wellington are respectfully informed, that a PUBLIC MEETING will be held at the **Britannia Saloon, on Friday Even.,** The 5th Day of August, 1853, To hear the opinion of all the candidates on several important questions. All the Candidates for the Representation of this City, of whatever Political opinion, are requested to attend.

THE CHAIR WILL BE TAKEN AT 7 O'C...

Wellington, August 2, 1853.

Notice of a meeting for electoral candidates in Wellington, 1853.

Eliza was just seven years old when there was great excitement, not just in her house, or even her town, but in the whole country. Her father was going off to vote in New Zealand's very first General Election!

Eliza ran to the front window and watched him walk down the path on his way to the polling station. He was dressed in his best clothes.

'Why aren't you voting too?' she asked her mother. 'I'm not allowed,' her mother replied. Eliza dreamed of being able to vote.

5

E whitu tau te pakeke o Raiha i te wā o te hari nui, kaua i tōna whare anake, i tōna tāone anake rānei, ēngari puta noa i te motu. Ko te pūtake o te hari nui, e whai wāhi ana tōna matua ki te pōti, i roto i te pōtitanga tuatahi o Aotearoa!

Ka oma a Raiha ki mua o te matapihi, kia kite a ia i tōna matua e hīkoi atu ana ki te teihana pōti. E mau ana hoki i ōna pūeru pai.

'He aha koe i kore ai e pōti?' te pātai ki tōna whāea. 'E kore au e whakaaetia,' te whakautu a tōna māmā. E wawata ana a Raiha kia āhei ia ki te pōti.

Edward Hart's life as a bricklayer

Edward Hart, was a journeyman bricklayer. This meant he was an employed craftsman who could lay 100–150 bricks an hour on a plain wall. In the early 1800s a brick-laying apprenticeship took seven years before a person became a 'journeyman'. After many years of experience, they could become Master Bricklayers, highly skilled and making enough money to employ journeymen.

Bricklaying required physical endurance, a keen eye for keeping a brick wall straight, creativity, and a practical knowledge of construction techniques.

Bricks were made at several sites in the villages of Bearsted and Thurnham in Kent, as the main ingredients needed to make them were nearby. There was a good supply of Gault clay (which made a reddish-brown brick) and a wide deposit of the fine white sand needed. The brickfield where Edward worked in Ware Street, Thurnham can be traced back to at least 1560, but finally closed down in around the 1920s.

Bricks were usually only laid in the spring and summer, so Edward had to look for other work in the off seasons. He found extra work digging and clearing fields, but life was tough for the Hart family. Wood, used for heating and cooking had to be gathered. Bearsted and Thurnham had access to fresh water from wells fed by springs, but lanterns and candles were a luxury, a vegetable garden a necessity and, if lucky, the family had a pig and chickens. Eggs could be sold and acorns gathered by the children to feed a pig, whose preserved meat would help feed the family through the long cold winter.

As towns and cities grew in colonial New Zealand, bricklayers were needed to construct buildings. Bricks were a common material for early commercial buildings, especially larger ones in Auckland and Wellington. There was a lot of work for bricklayers, not just on buildings, but also for lining wells and tunnels and building chimneys for wooden houses. In Wellington bricklayers put up large stores, churches and a hospital, but many brick buildings collapsed in the earthquakes of 1848 and 1855, and much rebuilding was done using wood.

Sticking bricks together

Lime mortar was first used about 6,000 years ago. Bricklayers like Edward Hart made it from limestone to stick their bricks together. Limestone is found in ancient seabeds and formed over centuries as corals, shellfish and lime-producing plants were squeezed together. Burning limestone (which has to be done carefully as it gives off poison gas) produces a white powder – quicklime – which is added to water to cause a chemical reaction. This process is called slaking. The slaked lime is then mixed with sand to create lime mortar, a paste that is workable, slow drying and durable.

Old bricks at the site of Thurnham Brickfield.

Unsanitary and overcrowded housing, low wages, poor diet, unemployment and sickness affected ordinary people like the Hart family, who like millions of others, emigrated to seek a better life.

Steerage class on the New Zealand Company ship *Tyne*

The Hart family were granted free passage on board the *Tyne*, which left England from Gravesend in northwest Kent on 25 March 1841. They had very little space or privacy on board and families probably slept in a corner with two bunks, one on top of the other. Luggage was stored down in the hold, their bunk space only allowing a small bag. Fresh water was for drinking only; for anything else a bucket of seawater was used. The New Zealand Company provided provisions, mattresses and bolsters, and cooking utensils but the emigrants had to bring blankets, sheets and covers, as well as towels, cutlery, tin or pewter plates and drinking mugs. Men had to bring two complete suits of exterior clothing, two pairs of shoes, and six changes of shirts and stockings. Women needed six shifts, two flannel petticoats, six pairs of stockings, two pairs of shoes and two strong gowns.

After four months at sea the Hart family arrived in Wellington, anchoring off Kaiwarra as there was no wharf at Port Nicholson. A basket lowered passengers into a boat and sailors rowed them ashore to their new lives. The *Tyne* made three voyages to New Zealand, but on 3 July 1845 sailed into a fierce storm and hit rocks. With the cabins underwater and the bulkheads destroyed, she capsized two days later.

THE EMIGRANTS' COOK

On the voyage to New Zealand in 1841, Edward Hart was the emigrants' cook. It was tricky lighting fires and cooking for people on board a ship, especially during rough weather when the rolling motion would throw everything about. Steerage passengers like the Harts, cooked and ate in a communal area with a long table and benches either side. Their own lamps, bags, pots, mugs and provisions would have hung from rows of hooks on the ceiling. The shipboard diet included salted meats (beef and pork), bread, pease (lentils and other legumes) and oatmeal, with little if any fresh food.

Port Nicholson, Wellington
by Charles Heaphy, 1841.

Immigration Department.

CLASSIFIED list of immigrants brought to Wellington at the expense of the New Zealand Company, in the barque *Tyne*, 500 tons, Captain Robertson, from London.

	Male.	Female.	Total.
Adults, married	15	15	30
Do., single	16	13	29
	31	28	59
Children 7 to 14 years			17
Do. 1 to 7			7
Do. under 1			3
Total			86

	Married.	Single.	Total.
Agricultural Labourer	1	6	7
Boot Makers	1	1	2
Bricklayers	1	1	2
Carpenter	1	1	2
Gardener	1	0	1
Glazier	0	1	1
Labourer	6	4	10
Mason	0	1	1
Miner	3	0	3
Sawyer	1	0	1
Smith	0	1	1
	15	16	31
Sempstress		11	
Servant		1	12
Total			43

D. RIDDIFORD,
Immigration Agent.

August 9, 1841.

THE undersigned have on sale, ex *Tyne* and other late arrivals,

Anchors, chains and cables of all sizes and dimensions, and of superior manufacture, and guaranteed,
Prime India and Irish mess beef and pork in tierces and barrels,
Paints, oils, turps, sheet lead,
Coals, Newcastle grindstones, fire bricks and clay,
Raisins, currants, Dutch cheese, hams, soap,
Windows, flint and cut glass and earthenware in great variety,
Wines, brandy, Geneva, East and West India rum,
Bar and bolt sheet and rod iron,
Whaling gear of every description,
Whale lines, Europe and coir rope, twines, &c.
600 pipe staves,
Preserved meats—salmon, grouse, venison, &c. &c.
Truman and Taylor's brown stout and ale in cask and bottle,
Claret, Hermitage, Chablis, &c., in 1 dozen cases,
Clothing and slops, hosiery, blankets, prints, and flannel,
Muskets, flints, ironmongery of every sort,
Superior corn mills,
Shingle, batten, paling, and spike nails, pit and cross-cut saws,
Hats, caps, and ladies' bonnets,
Linens, diapers, damask table covers, doilies, and napkins,
Tar, pitch, black and brown varnish,
Weights, scales, steelyards, shot,
Refined sugar, wine corks, stationery,
1 case india-rubber clothing,
Superfine and pilot cloths, cashmeres,
1 case assorted snuffs, tobacco,
Bandannas and Turkey red handkerchiefs, Swiss sewings,
Pickles, mustard, vinegar, bottled fruits, and sauces,
Ink, blacking,
Floor cloth all sizes,
2 cases ladies' shoes, 1 case men's strong do., 1 case ladies' stays,
Furniture, white feathers.

Eliza was her family's first New Zealander, born in Wellington in 1846. Her parents, older sisters and brother had spent over 19 weeks on board a ship to reach Aotearoa. They arrived in 1841, the year after the Treaty of Waitangi was signed.

Life was tough in this new country, but Eliza had heard the family stories about how much worse it was back in England. Her father was a bricklayer, and in England could only get work during summer when it was dry. The rest of the year he did odd jobs, such as gathering in harvests.

Ko Raiha te mema tuatahi o tōna whānau i whānau mai ki tēnei motu, i Te Whanganui-a-Tara i te 1846. 19 wiki te roa o tōna whānau i runga kaipuke, ōna mātua, ōna tuākana me tōna tūngane, kia tae mai rātau ki Aotearoa. I ū mai i te 1841, kotahi tau i muri i te hainatanga o te Tiriti o Waitangi.

He uaua te noho i tēnei whenua hou, ēngari kua rongo kē a Raiha i ngā kōrero mō te uaua kē atu o te noho i Inarangi. He hora pereki te mahi a tōna matua, ēngari i Inarangi ka mahi noa ia i te raumati i te wā e maroke ana. I ētahi atu wā, he poka noa te mahi, pēnei i te hauhake kai.

Prison Hulks

Unseaworthy ships became floating prisons in the 18th and 19th centuries. Conditions on board the prison hulks were bad. Convict William Derricourt wrote, 'Before going on board we were stripped to the skin and scrubbed with a hard scrubbing brush . . . the hair was clipped from our heads as close as scissors could go . . . the blood was drawn in many places. Our next experience was being marched off to the blacksmith, who riveted on our ankles rings of iron connected by eight links to a ring in the centre, to which was fastened an up and down strap or cord reaching to the waist-belt. This last supported the links, and kept them from dragging on the ground. Then we had what were called knee garters. A strap passing from them to the basils [iron ring encircling each ankle] and buckled in front and behind caused the weight of the irons to traverse on the calf of the leg.' Rowed off the hulks in gangs at dawn, the convicts worked under guard until dusk, their poor quality clothing quickly became filthy and ragged.

EDWARD HART: CONVICT

- **1827 (Sept 1):** Edward is taken on board the *Retribution* which is moored on the River Medway near Sheerness. Convict James Hardy Vaux wrote, 'There were confined in this floating dungeon nearly 600 men, most of them double ironed; and the reader may conceive the horrible effects arising from the continual rattling of chains, the filth and vermin naturally produced by such a crowd of miserable inhabitants.'

- **1827 (Sept 20):** Edward's family express 'sorrow and misery' at hearing that he may be transported, begging for him to stay in his 'native land'. The family's request was refused.

- **1828 (Nov 1):** From Feb–Oct 1828 the *Weymouth* is fitted out as a convict ship. Edward is moved on board and transported when the ship sails for Bermuda on 4 Jan 1829. Convict labour from England's prison hulks fills a labour shortage as the Royal Engineers build dockyards and fortifications on Ireland Island in Bermuda for the British Royal Navy. The *Weymouth* anchors offshore to house convicts who are young and fit, usually convicted of larceny, and serving a lesser term of seven years, just like Edward. Bermuda was one of the most brutal British convict outposts. Of 9,000 convicts sent there between 1824–1863, some 2,000 died from illness or accident. Back-breaking work at Bermuda included quarrying limestone to build a massive breakwater to protect the dockyards from waves.

- **1831 (Nov 21):** Edward dictates a letter asking for mercy which includes a good conduct letter from the Acting Overseer of the *Weymouth*.

- **1832 (Mar 6):** A petition on Sarah Hart's behalf states, 'it was her husband's first offence . . . she is left with two small children to provide for who with herself in consequence of this unfortunate affair are reduced to the most abject state of misery and wretchedness and reluctantly compelled to become a burden on their Parish for support'. Edward is transported back to England to the *Discovery* moored at Deptford Dockyard.

- **1833 (Jul 1):** Edward is on board the *Ganymeade* moored near Woolwich when he receives a Free Pardon after serving six years. Edward and Sarah's next child is born in October 1834.

View near Woolwich in Kent showing the employment of the convicts from the hulks, c. 1800.

'Our next experience was being marched off to the blacksmith, who riveted on our ankles rings of iron connected by eight links to a ring in the centre.'

The dockyard under construction on Ireland Island, Bermuda and four prison hulks. The hill towards the left was levelled by quarrying, 1848.

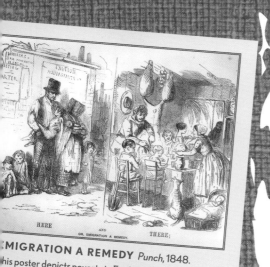

EMIGRATION A REMEDY *Punch, 1848.*
This poster depicts poverty in England compared with life in New Zealand, the 'land of plenty'. Around a quarter of the population in Britain at the time lived in poverty and faced unsanitary and overcrowded housing, low wages, poor diet, insecure employment and the effects of sickness and old age. Millions of ordinary people like the Hart family looked to emigration to escape poverty and make a better life.

EMIGRATION
TO
NEW ZEALAND.

The Directors of the New Zealand Company, do hereby give notice that they are ready to receive Applications for a **FREE PASSAGE** to the
TOWN OF WELLINGTON,
AT LAMBTON HARBOUR,
PORT NICHOLSON, COOK'S STRAITS,
NEW ZEALAND,
From Agricultural Laborers, Shepherds, Miners, Gardeners, Brickmakers, Mechanics, Handi-craftsmen, and Domestic Servants, **BEING MARRIED**, and not exceeding Forty years of age; also from **SINGLE FEMALES**, under the care of near relatives, and **SINGLE MEN**, ac-companied by one or more **ADULT SISTERS**, not exceeding, in either case, the age of Thirty years. Strict inquiry will be made as to qualifi-cations and character.
Apply on Mondays, Thursdays, and Satur-days, to Mr. JOSEPH PHIPSON, 11, Union Passage, Birmingham,
AGENT TO THE COMPANY.
TOWN and **COUNTRY SECTIONS** of **LAND** on sale, full particulars of which may be had on application as above.

"BULK "DROMEDARY." NEW VICTUALLING-STORES BUILDING. KEEP AND COMMISSIONER'S HOUSE.

Eliza's older sister told her about one time in England when their father had no work at all. Their mother was about to have another baby and no work meant no food. Eliza's father stole some food to feed his family. He was caught and sent to jail on board an old wreck of a ship for six years!

After he was released, Eliza's parents looked for a better life for their family. When they saw free tickets to New Zealand, they jumped at the chance to move to a healthy new country, where there was enough work, and food for their growing family.

9

I kōreo atu te tuakana o Raiha ki a ia mō te wā kāore he mahi a tōna matua. Nā, i te hapū hoki tō rātau whāea, ā, kāore he kai mō te whānau. He whānako kai te mahi a tōna matua hei whāngai i tōna whānau. Ka mau ia, ka whiua ki runga i te kaipuke herehere mō te ono tau!

Nō tana putanga i te herehere, ka kimi ngā mātua o Raiha kei hea he oranga mō te whānau. Nō te kitenga he kore utu ētahi tīkiti ki Aotearoa, kāore te whānau i ārikarika ki te hūnuku ki whenua haumako, ki whenua nui te mahi, ki whenua makuru i te kai.

ELECTION DAY IN MASTERTON 26 SEPTEMBER 1887

Most early New Zealand politicians were from the wealthy colonial elite. Māori men gained full suffrage rights when four Māori seats were created in 1867. Universal male suffrage was granted in 1879 when all adult Pākehā men over 21, whether they owned property or not, could vote in the eighth General Election on 8–9 December 1881. Voting in more than one electorate was seen as unfair and in 1889 the 'one man, one vote' policy started. More working men become involved in politics as a result.

'The change is coming, but why is New Zealand only to follow? Why not take the initiative?'
Femmina, 18 August 1869

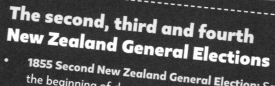

The second, third and fourth New Zealand General Elections

- **1855 Second New Zealand General Election:** Said to be the beginning of democracy in New Zealand as it was the first one which elected a Parliament that had full authority to govern the colony. There were no political parties in New Zealand, instead all candidates were independents.

- **1860–61 Third New Zealand General Election:** Gold miners who held a Miner's Right continuously for at least three months were now able to vote without having to own, lease or rent property. The verbal voting system introduced in 1858 meant the elector said out loud the name of the candidate he was voting for and the polling official wrote the name in a poll book beside which the elector signed his name.

- **1866 Fourth New Zealand General Election:** The Māori Representation Act 1867 created four Māori seats compared to 72 Pākehā seats. The first Māori elections for these seats were held in 1868, with Māori males over 21 gaining the right to vote. Māori elections were then held as part of the General Elections.

- **1871 Fifth New Zealand General Election:** The first in which the secret ballot was used instead of the verbal voting system, which meant a voter's choice was anonymous and less open to vote buying, intimidation or blackmail. The voting paper was then deposited in a locked ballot box.

Marriage of Eliza Hart and John Wallis, 1863

Eliza Hart married John Wallis on 13 January 1863. After marriage, women became their husband's property, along with any money they made, gifts or inheritance. A woman's legal identity became that of her husband and she had no right to a share of his earnings or estate, even after he died.

Eliza's marriage certificate shows that she was a minor when she married and her father, Edward Hart, signed his name as a witness with an X meaning that he was unable to read and write.

John Wallis is thought to have been born in Chatham, Kent, in 1839. It is believed that John went to sea with the Navy and then 'jumped ship' in New Zealand where he established himself as a carpenter by trade. It is not known whether he supported women's suffrage. John died in Christchurch on 27 May 1903.

John Wallis

Purification, *New Zealand Graphic*, 18 November 1893. This cartoon shows the 'dirty boy' of politics being scrubbed clean by a woman using a firm hand and water from a bucket labelled 'Woman's Vote'.

Dirty Politics

Early New Zealand elections were held on working days with polls only open from 9am–4pm. The largest electorates often had only one or two polling booths and some voters travelled for days on horseback to reach one. Settlers often couldn't afford the time away from their farms.

At the polling booths, often located in taverns, candidates could offer free alcohol in return for a vote. Claims of bribery and bullying were made as a number of electoral rolls overflowed with false entries. Some electors voted under more than one name, and there were entries from people known to have died! Large, unruly crowds gathered and candidates hired musicians, flew banners, and organised parades and lavish banquets. Drunken people staggering about the streets were dragged into polling booths to record their votes.

After the polls closed on election night, crowds gathered to hear the returning officer announce the local results. Groups of young men often threw eggs, rotten fruit, flour bombs or firecrackers, and drunken scuffles were common.

In 1858 a series of reform acts were passed to counter dirty politics. Candidates were banned from bribery, employing musicians and displaying banners, and polling booths were no longer allowed in taverns.

However, politics was still a dirty business and first-wave feminists argued that women's votes would clean up politics and help to usher in good government and necessary reforms. In 1893 conduct at the polling booth for women's first chance at voting was orderly and organised. This was thought to be as a result of women's civilising influence. Most candidates quickly cleaned up their act, realising that they needed the women's vote.

As Eliza grew up she watched her father go off to vote in the second and third General Elections. When she was 16, she married and had a little girl of her own, but she was still not allowed to vote.

In the fourth election, Eliza's husband went off to vote with the other men. Eliza looked at her little daughter, Emily, and promised her that one day they would both have the right to vote for the government of the country.

Ia Raiha e tipu ana, i kite ia i tōna matua e haere atu ana ki te pōti, i te pōtitanga tuarua, tautoru hoki o te motu. Ka eke ki te 16 ōna tau, ka moe tāne, ā, ka whānau mai tana tamāhine, ēngari kāore tonu ia e whakaaetia ki te pōti.

Nō te pōtitanga tuawhā, ka haere te hoa tāne o Raiha ki te pōti me ōna hoa. Ka tiro iho a Raiha ki tana kōtiro a Ēmere me te oati atu ki a ia, tērā anō te rā e āhei ai rāua ki te pōti.

Women's Christian Temperance Union

By 1879, colonial New Zealand had one pub for every 287 people and death was said to be most common from 'drink, drowning, and drowning while drunk'.

The first international women's society in New Zealand was the Women's Christian Temperance Union (WCTU), established in 1885 in response to the major social problem of alcohol abuse. Eliza was a member of the group, whose first national convention was held in 1886. Large numbers of women joined temperance organisations, probably because they were the most common victims of men's binge drinking.

There was a pub on every corner where many husbands drank away their pay packet. Drunkenness often resulted in violence towards women and children.

People were urged to 'sign the pledge' to not drink, and Parliament came under pressure to ban the production and consumption of alcohol. The WCTU campaigned strongly for women's political rights as it was felt that once they had the vote, women could change the liquor laws.

Eliza is last recorded as being a member of the WCTU in 1913 when she was part of a group representing the Christchurch branch at the 8th annual convention in Ashburton.

The Council was an opportunity for women to gather together, listen to papers on serious societal problems, debate the issues, and advocate for solutions.

What, dinner not ready yet! What have you been doing? *New Zealand Mail* 1893.

This typical anti-suffrage cartoon warns that tampering with men and women's 'natural' gender roles could lead to the breakdown of society — as represented by screaming babies, burnt dinner and cats in the milk jug.

Canterbury Women's Institute

In September 1892 Eliza was a founding member of the feminist group, the Canterbury Women's Institute (CWI). The CWI spearheaded the suffrage campaign in Canterbury and, being secular and non-temperance, attracted a wider membership than the WCTU.

The CWI supported the women's suffrage campaign and issues such as equal pay, divorce, old age pensions and the ending of capital punishment. They also worked for the election of women to public boards and committees. Although the first-wave feminists won the vote in 1893, it would be another 26 years before the Women's Parliamentary Rights Act would give them the right to stand for election. In the meantime, women were barred from effective participation in politics and government. This restricted their ability to achieve legal changes to create a better world.

Eliza was serving on the CWI committee in April 1896 when they held a conference in Christchurch, during which the National Council of Women was formed. She was still a committee member in 1910.

National Council of Women 'Women's Parliament'

On 17 February 1896 the CWI proposed a national convention of women's groups be held, called the National Council Of Women (NCW). An invitation was given to the women of New Zealand to attend. The convention was held at the Provincial Council Chambers in Christchurch from 13–18 April. Delegates from 11 women's groups throughout the country attended and together formed the National Council of Women, with Kate Sheppard as their first president.

Often referred to as the 'Women's Parliament', the council was an opportunity for women to gather together, listen to papers on serious societal problems, debate the issues, and advocate for solutions.

TEMPERANCE DEMONSTRATION IN PITT STREET, AUCKLAND ON ELECTION DAY 25 NOVEMBER 1902

NOTICE TO EPICENE WOMEN
NOVEMBER 1902

Printed by Wellington money lender and debt-collector Henry Charles Clarke Wright, this poster urges women to go home, look after the children, cook their husband's dinners, empty the slops, and generally attend to the domestic affairs for which nature designed them. Wright used epicene to mean that women involved in politics had masculine characteristics. Other copies of this notice were likely printed prior to universal suffrage being granted in 1893.

Emily Townsend (née Wallis)

The 1893 and 1896 New Zealand Electoral Rolls show Emily Wallis was living with Kate Sheppard at 83 Clyde Road in Riccarton. The 1900 Electoral Roll shows that she had moved back to her parents at 19 Ensors Road in Ōpāwa, and was working as a nurse. Emily married widower Abraham Townsend the following year. She sent this postcard in nurses uniform to her younger brother Leonard for Christmas 1910, when she would have been about 47.

Years passed and Emily grew and had a baby of her own. Eliza now had 10 children as well Emily's baby to look after. When the family moved from Wellington to Christchurch, Eliza met other women, along with some men, who also believed that women should have the right to vote.

The women gave out flyers, put up posters, gave talks, and organised petitions calling on Parliament to let the women vote. They knocked on hundreds of doors gathering signatures for their petitions. Many doors were slammed in their faces!

13

Ka ngaro ngā tau, ka tipu a Ēmere, ā, ka whānau tana tamaiti ake. 10 rawa ngā tamariki a Raiha i taua wā, ā, me te tiaki hoki i tana mokopuna. Nō te hūnukutanga o te whānau i Te Whanganui-a-Tara ki Ōtautahi, ka rokohanga e Raiha ētahi atu wāhine, me ētahi tāne, e whakapono ana me āhei te wahine ki te pōti.

Tohaina haeretia e ngā wāhine nei ētahi pānui, ka whakairitia ētahi karere, ka kauhau, ā, ka whakaritea ētahi petihana ki te Pāremata kia whakamanatia te wahine ki te pōti. E hia rau kuaha i pātōtōtia ki te kohi waitohu mō ngā petihana. He nui tonu hoki ngā kuaha i katia wawetia!

Emily Wallis and daughter Esther

Emily was a 15-year-old pupil teacher at Colombo Road School in Christchurch when she became pregnant to a fellow student. She was sent to the Female Refuge in Stanmore Road which opened in 1876 as a home, maternity hospital and adoption agency for pregnant women. Emily turned 16 two months before she gave birth to her daughter, Esther, on 8 October 1879. The Female Refuge records indicate that Emily and Esther were both unwell following the birth:

7 Oct: Female infant, very weakly and constantly ailing, mother unable to suckle it.

8 Oct: Emily Wallis ill with fever.

7 Nov: E. Wallis left the Refuge to go as Housemaid to Mrs Heywood at £20 a year. Her child has been adopted by some friends. Since the adoption of her child her parents have received her.

Remarks: This was a very sad case, the girl being only 16 and the father 19, a lad attending the school where she was a pupil teacher. She had parents living at Ōpāwa who were in great distress at the discovery of their daughter's condition, but their small home and large family prevented the possibility of her being confined at home.

Esther's first placement must have fallen through as Emily's parents (Esther's grandparents) Eliza and John Wallis, raised her until she turned 10. Esther was then adopted by Minnie Dean.

Esther Wallis Dean and the rest of the children taken after Charles and Minnie Deans' arrest at their home in East Winton, known as The Larches (1895).
From left: Ethel Maud Hay, Florence Smith, Esther Wallis with 'Baby Gray', Cecil Guilford and Arthur Wilson.

Minnie Dean

WILLIAMINA IRENE DEAN (NÉE MCCULLOCH). Born in Scotland on 2 September 1844, Minnie's mother and three sisters died before she was 13. Minnie moved to Tasmania, Australia, where she had two illegitimate children. Arriving in New Zealand in 1868, she claimed to be the widow of a doctor. Minnie taught at various schools before moving to Nightcaps in Southland. Nearby was Dunrobin Station where Charles Dean worked as a shepherd. On 19 June 1872 they married at his home in Etal Creek. In 1880 they adopted five-year-old Margaret Cameron. On 6 August 1882 Minnie's daughter Ellen, likely suffering from post-natal depression, drowned herself and her two children in their home well at Woodlands. In 1884 Charles was declared bankrupt and in c.1887 they moved to 'The Larches' in Winton where Minnie began taking in unwanted babies for money.

In October 1889 a six-month-old baby died of convulsions after a three-day illness, then in March 1891 a six-week-old infant died of inflammation of the heart valves and congestion of the lungs. An inquest told Minnie to improve the children's living conditions, but another baby died six weeks later. The 1893 Infant Life Protection Act stated that homes receiving payment for looking after infants under the age of two for more than three days in a row had to be licensed as foster homes and were subject to police inspection.

Four-year-old Willie Phelan is thought to have drowned at The Larches, around November 1893. Margaret and Esther Wallis would later testify that 'Mrs Dean did not treat this child well. She would knock him down and seize him by the hair and bump his head on the floor. Mrs Dean was in the habit of getting drunk, but was always sober when she abused the child'. Minnie buried Willie's body in the garden. On 2 May 1895 she was seen boarding a train carrying a young baby and a hat-box, then later carrying only the hat-box. A police search in The Larches' garden unearthed the bodies of two babies and the skeleton of Willie Phelan.

Charles and Minnie were arrested in 1895 with six children in their care. All were healthy but poorly dressed and living in squalor. Margaret (aged 19) and Esther (aged 15) looked after the children until the police placed them in a Charitable Aid Board home in Invercargill. The girls had to identify the bodies recovered from The Larches and give evidence at Minnie's trial. Charles was discharged without conviction, but is reported to have tried to frighten Esther into changing her testimony.

Minnie was found guilty of infanticide on 21 June 1895. She was hanged at Invercargill Prison on 12 August 1895, a much harsher sentence than would be given out today. Minnie was the first and only New Zealand woman to receive the death penalty and be hanged. She was buried in Winton Cemetery and in 1896 the Infant Protection Act extended police powers of inspection. Minnie's story exposed the stark realities of paid childcare and the lack of choice that many women faced.

illegitimate children in the 1880s died at more than double the rate of other children

'Fallen women' in New Zealand

Historically, pregnancy outside of marriage was frowned upon and thought to be a major threat to public decency. Contraception was not readily available and abortion could be fatal.

Some 'fallen women' were sent in disgrace to homes for unmarried mothers where they gave birth, often never seeing their newborn baby. Charitable Aid Boards and the state would not assist unmarried mothers to keep their babies.

Children born outside of marriage were said to be 'illegitimate' because they had no legal father and were not entitled to paternal support or inheritance.

The difficulties facing single mothers and their unwanted children often saw children adopted out or placed in orphanages, with baby farmers such as Minnie Dean, or in children's homes and industrial schools. Illegitimate children died at more than double the rate of other children.

Children at Saint Saviour's Orphanage, Christchurch.

Eliza had another baby, and as the family lived in a small house, she couldn't look after her granddaughter Esther any longer. Her daughter Emily didn't have the means to support her child.

Emily searched for a nice couple to look after her daughter. She found Minnie and Charles Dean who wanted an older child, and adopted 10-year-old Esther in 1890, the same year as the 11th New Zealand General Election.

15

Ka whānau mai he pēpi hou, ā, nā te pakupaku o tō rātau kāinga kāore i taea e ia te tiaki i tana mokopuna a Esther. Kāore hoki he moni a Ēmere ki te tiaki i tana tamaiti.

Ka kimi haere a Ēmere i tētahi tokorua hei tiaki i tana tamaiti. Kitea rawatia e ia a Minnie rāua ko Charles Dean, ā, ka whāngaitia e rāua te tamaiti nei, 10 tau tōna pakeke, i te tau 1890, te tau tonu tērā o te pōtitanga 11 o Aotearoa.

The introduction of the modern bicycle in the 1880s opened up entirely new opportunities for women . . .

The status of Māori women

During the reign of Queen Victoria (1837–1901), British women had very little rights. Power and privilege rested in the hands of men as head of the household. This attitude arrived in New Zealand with Pākehā settlers.

Traditionally, Māori women inherited land rights and maintained control over their land. Wāhine rangatira (women of chiefly rank) held powerful positions. Some signed the Treaty of Waitangi in 1840 and argued cases in the Land Court once it was established in 1862. This status was eroded by British patriarchy, and further undermined by the Native Lands Act 1865 and the 1873 amendment.

Te Kotahitanga (the Māori Parliament) first met on 13 June 1892. Māori women could speak, but not vote or stand as members. This was challenged by suffragists Meri Te Tai Mangakāhia and Ākenehi Tōmoana. On 18 May 1893, Meri put a motion before Te Kotahitanga asking for these rights. Her speech highlighted Māori women's concern about loss of control over their own property, but the motion was not debated. In 1894 a bill passed allowing women to create committees. These led to the first national Māori organisation, Te Rōpū Wāhine Māori Toko i te Ora (Māori Women's Welfare League) in 1951. Māori women did not win the right to vote in Te Kotahitanga elections until 1897, and were never granted the right to stand as candidates.

Māori and Pākehā women had similar concerns, such as the effect of alcohol abuse, but Māori women also discussed the effect of colonisation on their people, including land loss and the lack of recognition of Māori women's rights as the owners of land and resources. On the Women's Suffrage Petition of 1893, just six Māori women have been identified, but there are possibly more who used an anglicised name or that of their husband. Women first voted in the Māori electorates on 20 December 1893.

The 1919 Women's Parliamentary Rights Act gave women the right to stand for Parliament, but it wasn't until 1935 that the first Māori woman stood as a candidate and 1949 when the first Māori woman was elected.

Bicycles, rational dress & knickerbockers

Women's quest for the vote was part of a wider change in thinking about the roles of women and men. The introduction of the modern bicycle in the 1880s opened up entirely new opportunities for women and challenged traditional beliefs about femininity.

Cycling was a highly political activity, and bicycles a symbol of freedom of movement and independence. At a cost of about £22, they were cheaper than buying and looking after a horse, easier to learn to ride, and didn't take an hour to get ready in order to go out! Women were no longer dependant on a man for transportation, were free to come and go, and could enjoy the thrill of speed while travelling four times faster than walking. Mobility meant greater participation in politics, education, work and recreation.

On 18 August 1892, a group of Christchurch women formed the Atalanta Cycling Club, the first all-women's cycling club in the world. Cycling in groups was safer as some women cyclists had reported abuse and jeering, as well as stones and food being thrown at them, sticks thrust into their spokes causing them fall off, and being pushed off their bicycles.

Traditional clothing was a danger for cyclists as skirts could catch in spokes and chains. The Society for Rational Dress started in London in 1881 and encouraged practical and comfortable clothing for women. New Zealand newspapers reported on the society and some women, especially cyclists, adopted the new and outrageous, but practical clothing. Bulky long skirts, heavy undergarments and tightly-laced, shape-altering corsets, were replaced by a divided cycling skirt or, for the more daring, a less fitted bodice and some form of knickerbockers (baggy, knee-length trousers).

Māori women dress reformers, Christchurch, 1906.

New Zealand Suffrage Centennial Medal, 1993

Established by Royal Warrant on 1 July 1993, the New Zealand Suffrage Centennial Medal was created to commemorate 100 years of women's suffrage in New Zealand. It also recognised New Zealand and Commonwealth citizens who had made a significant contribution to women's rights or issues in the country. The front of the bronze medal has Queen Elizabeth II, while the reverse has a fern and camellia flower curving around the words *1893 The New Zealand Suffrage Centennial 1993*, with both stems crossed at the bottom and tied with a bow. The striped ribbon in the New Zealand suffrage colours gold, white and violet. Gold for enlightenment and courage, white for purity of purpose, and violet for dignity and self-respect.

A Māori woman in rational dress with her bicycle. *New Zealand Graphic*, 1895.

By the time Eliza's 12th child was born in 1891, the suffragists had organised more petitions and gathered thousands of signatures.

Gold, white and violet were their colours. White camellias were given to suffrage supporters, while those who argued that women should never be allowed to vote but should get back to their kitchens, gave out red camellias.

Kia whānau rawa mai te tamaiti 12 a Raiha i te tau 1891, he nui tonu ngā petihana i whakaritea e ngā wāhine, ā e hia mano ngā waitohu.

Ko ngā tae he koura, he mā me te waiporoporo. He mea toha te kamēria mā ki te hunga tautoko i te pōti wahine. He nui tonu te hunga i tohe ko te wāhi tika mō te wahine ko te kāuta, nō reira hei aha mā rātau te mana pōti, ā, he kamēria whero tā rātau tohu.

1893 Women's Suffrage Petitions
Te Petihana Whakamana Pōti Wahine

In 1893, thirteen petitions were presented to the House of Representatives asking for women's suffrage. Over February–July 1893 the names, addresses, and signatures of 31,872 women (and some men) aged over 21 had been collected. Twelve petitions have not survived, but the 'monster petition' with 25,521 signatures did. It was submitted on 28 July 1893, and presented to the House of Representatives on 11 August by pro-suffrage MP Sir John Hall.

Petition Timeline

1893 Kept in the records department of the Legislative Department in Parliament building's cellars where it was in danger from rats and dust.

1975 Displayed as part of an exhibition on women's achievements.

1985 Displayed during an exhibition at Hamilton and over two years filmed onto microfiche and indexed by a team from Masterton. Transcription finished in 1993.

1991 Petition added to the National Archives collection. The petition sheets were carefully separated into six small rolls which revealed more signatures. A custom-built acid free box was specially made to keep them safe.

1992 The sheets are sorted into their original order and conservators repair each nick and tear. After a two year microfilming project the petition is displayed in the Constitution Room at Archives New Zealand in Wellington.

1993 National Archives display of the petition to mark 100 years of women's suffrage in New Zealand.

2011 Archives New Zealand re-digitised the petition at a much higher resolution before launching an online database.

2017 (April 22): The 1835 Declaration of Independence of the United Tribes of New Zealand, the 1840 Treaty of Waitangi and the 1893 Women's Suffrage Petition are moved a few hundred metres up the road from Archives New Zealand in Mulgrave Street to the National Library of New Zealand in Molesworth Street, Wellington. Special crates were made for each of the fragile documents. The Treaty and Declaration crates were cloaked in kiwi feather kākahu from Te Papa, and the Suffrage Petition draped with a quilt made by National Council of Women members in 1988.

2017 (May 19): Governor-General Dame Reddy opened He Tohu (The Signs), a new permanent exhibition to house the three iconic documents. The petition is the most vulnerable document, with the most light-sensitive inks.

The Carpet Knight
New Zealand Graphic, 12 August 1893

On 11 August 1893 Sir John Hall unrolled the 25,521 signature Women's Suffrage Petition like a carpet in front of the House of Representatives. He asked his political colleagues whether they liked 'the pattern'. Legislation was passed giving women the vote in time for the 1893 General Election.

Taking care of the Suffrage Petition

The petition is a primary source, proof of New Zealand's leading role in the women's suffrage story. Historical documents like these allow us to touch the lives of people in the past and find out where they lived and what they thought about a certain issue. The petition is a taonga, and taking care of it for the future is important. Some of the things that make the petition challenging to look after include:

- Inferior quality types and sizes of paper amongst sheets of good quality machine-made rag paper
- A variety of coloured inks, crayon and pencil used by signatories
- Past researchers rolling and unrolling the petition, resulting in tears
- Unequal sizes of sheets meaning some stick out and are more prone to damage
- Sheets which were sewn together
- Animal glue used to glue sheets together breaking down with age and causing staining. This was replaced with conservation paper and wheat starch paste.

In 2011 the 'monster petition' was digitised by Archives New Zealand.

The Women's Suffrage Petition in 1985 just before restoration work started.

The White Ribbon

The White Ribbon was the first New Zealand newspaper to be owned and operated solely by women. The first issue was produced in May 1895 by the Women's Christian Temperance Union (WCTU). The paper didn't start until two years after the successful suffrage campaign due to lack of money.

Eliza helped produce the paper and in a list of attendees at the 1899 WCTU convention is listed as 'Mrs Wallis (White Ribbon paper)'.

Kate Sheppard was the first editor, and articles included up-to-date ideas in health, childcare, divorcee rights, nutrition, dress, ex-prisoners' rights, and equality within the marriage. The monthly paper continued until 1960.

Eliza and the others worked hard and gathered signatures on several more petitions. In 1893 they created a 'monster petition' made from 546 sheets of paper glued together. It was so big that a wheelbarrow was used to deliver it to the steps of Parliament in Wellington!

The monster petition was wrapped around a section of broom handle. When it was unrolled down the middle of Parliament's debating chamber, it hit the wall at the end with a dramatic thud.

Over 25,000 signatures demanded the right for women to vote.

Ka whakaheke werawera a Raiha mā ki te kohi waitohu i runga petihana. Nō te tau 1893 ka hangaia he 'petihana kātuarehe' e 546 pihi pepa te nui! Na te kaha nui mā te huripara rā anō e waha ki te ngā arapiki o te Pāremata i Pōneke!

He mea tākai te petihana kātuarehe nei i runga hānara purūma. Nō te horatanga o te petihana i te kautahanga o te whare pāremata, ka pā rawa ki te pakitara tawhiti ā tau rawa.

Neke atu i te 25 mano waitohu e whakahau ana kia āhei te wahine ki te pōti.

Women vote for the first time at a polling station in the tiny South Otago settlement of Tahakopa, 28 November 1893.

Victory: Women's Franchise Passed, 8 September 1893

Political cartoon showing a triumphant woman celebrating the passing of the Electoral Act giving women the right to vote.
The arms represent the different groups now seeking women's votes.

VICTORY
WOMEN'S FRANCHISE PASSED, SEPTEMBER 8TH, 1893.

Crowds on Brougham Street, New Plymouth, election day 1893. A group of people, including women, standing outside the Provincial Council building where polling was held.

NEW ZEALAND INTRODUCES WOMEN'S SUFFRAGE : "Female suffrage has made much greater headway in New Zealand than at home. Not only did the women exercise their new right at the recent general elections, but a member of the fair sex has been elected Mayor of Onehunga. The women at the Borough Council Chambers exhibited unmistakable signs of triumph during the morning's Poll, for in working hours they were in possession of the whole field"

Women had been able to vote in Local Body Elections since 1876 via the Municipal Corporations Act. In this engraving, women are gathering outside the Devonport Borough Council Chambers on 28 November 1893 for their first vote in a General Election. The following day they voted in the local-body polls and Elizabeth Yates (née Oman), was voted Mayor of Onehunga, the first woman Mayor in the British Empire.

General Election, 28 November 1893

Women cast their first votes in the New Zealand European electorates on Tuesday 28 November 1893. The mood was festive, and Election Day calm and orderly, unlike the drunkenness and brawls of previous years. Voting in the Māori electorates took place on 20 December 1893.

Finally, Parliament could no longer ignore the women's voices, and in September 1893 passed the Electoral Act. New Zealand became the first self-governing country in the world to give women the vote and became a world leader in women's suffrage.

Just two months later, over 100,000 women enrolled to vote in the 12th New Zealand General Election. Eliza proudly cast her ballot alongside her husband and eldest daughter Emily. Soon, she would become a founding member of the National Council of Women in New Zealand and continue her work for women's rights.

Katahi rawa te Pāremata i whai taringa ki te reo o ngā wāhine, ā, i te marama o Māhuru i te tau 1893 ka whakamanatia te Ture Pōti hou. Ka noho ko Aotearoa te whenua kāwanatanga tuatahi o te ao ki te whakamana i te pōti wahine, ā, ka noho hei tirohanga mā te ao.

E rua marama i muri mai, neke atu i ta 100 mano ngā wāhine i rēhita ki te pōti i roto i te pōtitanga 12 o Aotearoa. Poho kererū ana a Raiha ki te pōti i te taha o tana hoa tāne, me tana tamāhine hoki a Ēmere. Nō muri tata ka noho ia hei mema tuatahi o te Kaunihera o ngā Wāhine o Aotearoa ki te kōkiri i nga mahi mō te mana wahine.

Postcard to Eliza from Kate Sheppard

Eliza's husband John Wallis died, aged 64, on 27 May 1903. That same year Eliza received a postcard from fellow suffragist Kate Sheppard. Because of the content it is believed to have been sent sometime after John's death:

Postmark: Surbiton, 10:15 am, 1903.

Mrs. Wallis,

I am going to attend a National Convention of Women Workers in London this week — to agitate for the franchise — I have been asked to tell about New Zealand.

Reverse: Thank you for your kind letter. You must keep as bright as possible for the sake of the others — Mr. S and Douglas are both well. I am visiting Mrs May at present. Mr May has gone to New Zealand on business. Best Wishes, from K.W.S.

[Mr. S refers to Kate Sheppard's husband Walter Allen Sheppard, Douglas is their son].

Houses of Parliament. London.

Thank you for kind letter — You must keep as bright as possible for the sake of the others — Mr. S. & Douglas are both well — I am visiting Mrs May at present — Mr May has gone to New Zealand on business. Best wishes — from K. W. S.

POST CARD

THE ADDRESS ONLY TO BE WRITTEN HERE.

THIS SPACE MAY BE USED FOR COMMUNICATION. (Post Office Regulation.)

I am going to attend a National Convention of Women Workers in London this week - to agitate for the franchise - I have been asked to tell about New Zealand.

Mrs. Wallis.
Frasers Road,
Ferry Road.
Christchurch.
New Zealand.

Women approaching the polling booth at the Drill Hall in Rutland Street, Auckland, during the General Election on 6 December 1899.

'Let us hope the ladies of the red and white camellias may not meet for personal explanations'.

Linwood Cemetery, Christchurch

Linwood Cemetery is the fifth oldest surviving cemetery established in Christchurch. It opened in 1884, and was the first municipal cemetery of the Christchurch City Council. The cemetery was located on the outskirts of the city, bounded by Butterfield Avenue, Hay Street, Buckleys Road and McGregors Road. It was deliberately put there because it was assumed the population would remain small and so would be far away from the medical problems thought to be caused by cemeteries.

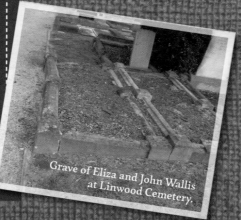

Grave of Eliza and John Wallis at Linwood Cemetery.

The White Camellia

The white camellia flower (*Camellia japonica alba plena*) became the symbol of the New Zealand women's suffrage movement after they were given to supporters in September 1893.

Camellia shrubs often produce masses of blooms in September, and this is likely why they were used by the suffragists. Today they are worn on Suffrage Day, 19 September, and also feature on the $10 note.

For the 1993 suffrage centennial Taranaki camellia breeders Viv Joyce and her father Alf Gamlin bred a special variety of white camellia. They named it 'Kate Sheppard' after the Christchurch feminist and suffrage leader.

Battle of the Buttonholes

On 12 September 1893 the suffragists presented a white camellia flower tied with a white ribbon to those members of the House of Representatives who had voted in favour of women gaining the vote. To counter that, on 6 September a basket of red camellia flowers were presented to an MP by a group of anti-suffrage women for those who voted against women's franchise. A reporter wrote, 'let us hope that the ladies of the red and white camellias may not meet'.

THE ORDER OF THE RED CAMELLIA.

Yesterday the Hon. W. C. Walker was presented with a basket of red camellias, to be distributed to those Legislative Councillors who opposed the women's franchise. This graceful presentation, which may be regarded as a counter to that which took place the other day, was accompanied with the following address :—" A committee of ladies of the city of Wellington respectfully request hon. members of the Legislative Council who spoke and voted against the franchise being granted to the women of the colony to accept this small token of their regard and esteem for their efforts to allow us to remain in our proper sphere apart from politics." I understand that some lady politicians of the other side express incredulity as to the genuineness of this presentation. Let us hope the ladies of the red and white camellias may not meet for personal explanations.

After having 12 children and working long and hard for women to have the same rights as men, Eliza died at her Christchurch home in 1914. It was one month after the start of the First World War and a few months before the 19th New Zealand General Election. Eliza died with the right to vote and the right of every New Zealand citizen to vote and have their voices heard.

Across her grave were scattered white camellias in memory of all she worked for.

23

I whakatipuhia e Raiha tana pā harakeke, i whakapau werawera hoki mō te mana o te wahine, kia rite ki ō te tāne, ā, kātahi ia ka mate i tōna kāinga i Ōtautahi i te tau 1914. He kotahi marama i muri mai o te pakarutanga o te riri i te Pakanga Tuatahi o te ao, e rua marama hoki, i mua o te pōtitanga 19 o Aotearoa. I mate a Raiha me tōna mana pōti, ā, ko tōna waihotanga tērā ki a tātau, kia whai mana ia tangata ki te pōti, kia rangona hoki ō rātau reo.

He mea ruirui ētahi kamēria mā ki tōna urupā hei tohu mahara mō āna mahi.

Women's Suffrage Petitions

Several petitions were circulated from 1884 in an effort to gain the right to vote for women, the last being the 'monster petition' of 1893. The suffrage petitions were the result of meetings in towns and cities across New Zealand, with women often travelling great distances to hear lectures and speeches, pass resolutions and, if aged 21 or over, sign petitions.

A century later, only two of the nationally important petitions dating from 1892 and 1893 are known to have survived. The loss or deliberate destruction of the others has created a gap in the history of New Zealand women, the unknown signatories part in the suffrage story lost to both their descendants and future researchers.

- **1891:** 8 petitions with more than 9,000 signatures
- **1892:** 6 petitions with almost 20,000 signatures
- **1893:** 13 petitions with 31,872 signatures including the 'monster petition' with 25,521 signatures

1892 Women's Suffrage Petition

The unsuccessful 1892 petition bears the signatures of more than 17,000 people, some living in areas not covered by the 'monster petition' the following year. Both Eliza and daughter Emily signed the 1892 petition, appearing on the database as names 418 and 419.

To the Honourable the Speaker and Members of the House of Representatives in Parliament assembled.

THE Petition of the undersigned Women, of the age of twenty-one years and upwards, resident in the Colony of New Zealand, humbly sheweth:—

THAT large numbers of Women in the Colony have for several years petitioned Parliament to extend the franchise to them.

THAT the justice of the claim, and the expediency of granting it, was, during the last Session of Parliament, affirmed by both Houses; but, that for reasons not affecting the principle of Women's Franchise, its exercise has not yet been provided for.

THAT if such provision is not made before the next General Election, your petitioners will, for several years, be denied the enjoyment of what has been admitted by Parliament to be a just right, and will suffer a grievous wrong.

THEY therefore earnestly pray your Honourable House to adopt such measures as will enable Women to record their votes for Members of the House of Representatives at the ensuing General Election.

THEY further pray that your Honourable House will pass no Electoral Bill which shall fail to secure to Women this privilege.

And your petitioners, as in duty bound, will ever pray, &c.

NAME.	ADDRESS.
Mary J. Carpenter	Yaldhurst
Annie Gilberthorpe	Yaldhurst
Susann Clarkson	Hornby
Julia F. Skelton	Hornby
Jane F. Smithie	Johnston
Isabella Chaplin	Templeton
Mary Hansen	Templeton
Louise Rosendale	Templeton
Priscilla Marshall	Templeton
Margaret Watson	Templeton
M. Ester Whaarte	Templeton
Jessie Cudsell	Templeton
Julia Najett	Templeton
Mary Jiffs	Templeton
Alice Holt	Riccarton
Emma Lambert	Hornby
R. W. Sheppard	Riccarton
K. Wallis	
J. Manson	"
J. Carleton	"
Jno Gulley	
S. W. Hawinson	Lyttelton
C. Hepburn	Fendalton
L. Hepburn	Riccarton
E. A. Perran	Fendalton
H. Pearl	Fendalton
F. Eare	Fendalton
L. Selwyn	Fendalton
E. Wallace	Fendalton
M. H. Denniston	Fendalton

THEY therefore earnestly pray your Honoura... to record their votes for Members of the House of Representatives at the ensuing General Election.

Sheet No. 532

Eliza's signature appears at the bottom of this sheet. At the time she was living at 49 Ensors Road, in Ōpāwa, Christchurch.

1893 'a monster petition'

Despite the failure of the 1892 petition, another was organised in 1893, described by Kate Sheppard as 'a monster petition'. Petition sheets were circulated throughout New Zealand then returned to Christchurch. Kate Sheppard glued the 546 individual pages together at her Clyde Road home. They formed a single roll stretching 274 metres long which was rolled around a section of broom handle. Today, some names and locations are illegible due to the varying light-sensitive inks some signatories used.

Sheet No. 1

The signature of Emily, Eliza's daughter, is directly underneath Kate Sheppard's on the first page of the petition, both of Riccarton, Christchurch. Evidence points to Emily living with Kate and her husband from 1893–1896.

Convention delegates & convenors outside the
Provincial Council Chambers, Christchurch, 13 April 1896.

Back row standing (from left):
1. Christine Kirk Henderson (1861–1953), CWI
2. Rose Claridge Atkinson (née Bell) (1872–1955), CWI

Second row (from left):
3. Emily Kinley Black (née Wilson) (1853–1939), CWI
4. Ellen Darling (née MacDean) (c.1858–1933), CWI
5. Lucy Masey Smith (1861–1936), CWI
6. Jessie Mackay (1864–1938), CWI
7. Eleanor Sarah Bruce Smith (née Dawson) (c.1863–1917), CWI
8. Eliza Wallis (née Hart) (1846–1914), CWI
9. Frances (Franc) Garstin (1866–1902), CWI
10. Annie Emma Hookham (later Taylor) (1856–1931), CWI

Third row (from left):
11. Susannah Isherwood (née Tanner) (1846–1915), Springfield Women's Institute
12. Amey Daldy (née Hamerton) (1829–1920, Auckland Women's Political Leagues
13. Wilhelmina Bain (née Sherriff) (1848–1944), President, CWI
14. Margaret Sievwright (née Richardson) (1844–1905), Gisborne Women's Political League
15. Kate Wilson Sheppard (née Malcolm) (1847–1934), CWI
16. Anna Paterson Stout (née Logan) (1858–1931), Wellington Southern Cross League
17. Annie Jane Schnackenberg (née Allen) (1835–1905), WCTU, Auckland
18. Sarah Ann Dorothy Izett (née Pattle) (1844–1929), Women's Liberal Association
19. Ada Jane Cooper (née Meynell) (1864–1917), Women's Christchurch Political League
20. Eleanor Phoebe Smith (née McLeod) (1828–1913), CWI

Front row (from left):
21. Ada Wells (née Pike) (1863–1933), Secretary, CWI
22. Jessie Marguerite Williamson (née McAllan) (1855–1937), Wanganui Women's Political League
23. Lucy Frances Ross (née Cross) (1864–?), Assistant Secretary CWI
24. Clara Maria Alley (née Buckingham) (1866–1952), Malvern Women's Institute
25. Emily Matilda Widdowson (née Lawrence) (1859–1915), WCTU, Christchurch

Eliza Wallis

A WOMEN'S PARLIAMENT

The Women's Convention, held at the suggestion of the Canterbury Women's Institute, was opened at 10a.m. today in the Provincial Council Chambers . . . the programme, which will extend over the entire week . . . was of national importance, and it might, without presumption, be said to be of world-wide significance. For the first time in our history the enfranchised women representing the political and social leagues of the colony were gathered together to consult on affairs of State policy . . .

Evening Star, 13 April 1896

Eliza Wallis

A portrait of the members of the Women's Council, formed at the Convention in Christchurch, 23 April 1896.

Standing (from left):
1. Susannah Isherwood (née Tanner) (1846–1915)
2. Clara Maria Alley (née Buckingham) (1866–1952)
3. Jessie Mackay (1864–1938)
4. Rose Claridge Atkinson (née Bell) (1872–1955)
5. Eliza Wallis (née Hart) (1846–1914)
6. Mary Smith (née Mounsey) (1862–1821)
7. Emily Kinley Black (née Wilson) (1853–1939)
8. Ann Agnes Ansell (c.1852–1936)
9. Frances (Franc) Garstin (1866–1902)

10. Jennie (Mary Jane) Smith (née Cumberworth) (1848–1924)
11. Eleanor Sarah Bruce Smith (née Dawson) (c.1863–1917)
12. Ada Jane Cooper (née Meynell) (1864–1917)
13. Ellen Darling (née MacDean) (c.1858–1933)
14. Sarah Ann Dorothy Izett (née Pattle) (1844–1929)

Second row (from left):
15. Annie Emma Hookham (later Taylor) (1856–1931)
16. Louisa Blake (née Lipscombe) (1844–1901)
17. Margaret Sievwright (née Richardson) (1844–1905)
18. Marion Ann Hatton (née Hanover) (1835–1905)

19. Kate Wilson Sheppard (née Malcolm) (1847–1934)
20. Annie Jane Schnackenberg (née Allen) (1835–1905)
21. Amey Daldy (née Hamerton) (1829–1920)
22. Marianne Allen Tasker (née Manchester) (1852–1911)

Seated on floor (from left):
23. Wilhelmina Bain (née Sherriff) (1848–1944)
24. Jessie Marguerite Williamson (née McAllan) (1855–1937)
25. Ada Wells (née Pike) (1863–1933)
26. Emily Matilda Widdowson (née Lawrence) (1859–1915)

NATIONAL COUNCIL OF WOMEN

'On the 13th of April, 1896, was forged one of those delicate golden chains which bind the earth together more firmly than ever did the iron shackles of conquest. On that day the Convention called together in Christchurch by the Canterbury Women's Institute, and composed of delegates from the different female societies throughout the country, formed itself into the National Council of the New Zealand women — a body which if not yet actually affiliated to the International Council, is bound by correspondence, sympathy, and unity of aim to that great cosmopolitan organisation.'

South Canterbury Times, 25 April 1896

Eliza Wallis

First meeting of the National Council of Women (NCW), Christchurch, April 1896.

Standing (from left):

1. Ann Agnes Ansell (née Ward) (c.1852–1936), Dunedin
2. Mary Smith (née Mounsey) (1862–1821), Christchurch
3. Annie Emma Hookham (later Taylor) (1856–1931), Christchurch
4. Lucy Frances Ross (née Cross) (1864–?), Christchurch
5. Jessie Mackay (1864–1938), Christchurch
6. Susannah Isherwood (née Tanner) (1846–1915), Christchurch
7. Emily Kinley Black (née Wilson) (1853–1939), Christchurch
8. Emily Matilda Widdowson (née Lawrence) (1859–1915), Christchurch
9. Frances (Franc) Garstin (1866–1902), Christchurch
10. Eliza Wallis (née Hart) (1846–1914), Christchurch
11. Ellen Darling (née MacDean) (c.1858–1933), Christchurch
12. Jessie Marguerite Williamson (née McAllan) (1855–1937), Wanganui
13. Agnes Wilson (1853–1925) Christchurch

Seated (from left):

14. Eleanor Sarah Bruce Smith (née Dawson) (c.1863–1917), Christchurch
15. Amey Daldy (née Hamerton) (1829–1920), Auckland
16. Marion Ann Hatton (née Hanover) (1835–1905), Dunedin, Vice-president
17. Anna Paterson Stout (née Logan) (1858–1931), Wellington, Vice-president
18. Kate Wilson Sheppard (née Malcolm) (1847–1934), Christchurch; President
19. Annie Jane Schnackenberg (née Allen) (1835–1905), Auckland, Vice-president
20. Margaret Sievwright (née Richardson) (1844–1905), Gisborne
21. Marianne Allen Tasker (née Manchester) (1852–1911), Wellington
22. Sarah Ann Dorothy Izett (née Pattle) (1844–1929), Christchurch, secretary

Seated on floor (from left):

23. Clara Maria Alley (née Buckingham) (1866–1952), Malvern
24. Ada Wells (née Pike) (1863–1933), Christchurch
25. Wilhelmina Bain (née Sherriff) (1848–1944), Christchurch

Eliza Wallis

Suratura Tea Supplement, *Otago Daily Times*

The temperance movement advocated drinking high-quality tea as a respectable, non-intoxicating and healthy alternative to alcohol, the 'demon drink'. In this sketch the National Council of Women are enjoying a cup of the 'Pure, Honest Ceylon' Suratura Tea, the 'Best Family Tea', 'guaranteed not blended with Indian, China, or any cheap or inferior teas'.

The blurb reads: 'The Suratura tea proprietary is most enterprising in their efforts to place before the homes of the people in New Zealand the very excellent qualities of the famous Suratura tea. They circulate through the STAR today a valuable pictorial supplement showing portraits of the 25 New Zealand ladies who composed the National Council of Women, held at Christchurch in April last. In the hand of each lady is held a cup of Suratura tea, which they are sipping with evident delight. The likenesses are very good'.

Auckland Star, 3 October 1896

Children of Eliza and John Wallis

1. **Emily Townsend (née Wallis) (1863–1914).** Born in Wellington on 23 August 1863. Pupil teacher at Colombo Road School in Christchurch. Illegitimate daughter, Esther, born 8 October 1879. Married Abraham Henry Townsend on 1 June 1901. Died in Linwood, Christchurch, on 6 March 1914.

2. **Herbert Wallis (1865–1865).** Born in Wellington on 14 March 1865. Died on 15 December 1865, aged nine months. Buried in Bolton Street Cemetery.

3. **John Wallis (1866–1868).** Born in Wellington on 27 December 1866. Died on 29 July 1868, aged 19 months. Buried in Bolton Street Cemetery.

4. **Frederick Arthur Wallis (1869–1920).** Born in Wellington on 24 November 1869. Never married but by 1895 in Sunnyside Lunatic Asylum. Died in Seaview Asylum at Hokitika on 8 September 1920.

5. **Alice Matilda Farquharson (née Wallis) (1872–1934).** Born in Wellington on 13 September 1872, she was a dressmaker. Married Christopher Farquharson on 26 December 1898. Died in Christchurch on 5 November 1934.

6. **Gertrude May Rickard (née Wallis) (1874–1955).** Born in Christchurch on 6 August 1874. She was a tailoress. Married George Warren Rickard on 26 December 1901. Died in Christchurch on 13 January 1955.

7. **Elizabeth Wallis (1877–1952) 'Edith'.** Born in Christchurch on 22 January 1877. Never married. Died in Wellington on 7 July 1952.

8. **Ellen Sarah Waller (née Wallis) (1879–1940).** Born in Christchurch on 26 April 1879. She was a machinist. Married James Robb Waller on 5 April 1915. Died in Christchurch on 16 February 1940.

9. **Frank Leonard Wallis (1882–1964).** Born in Christchurch on 13 February 1882. He was a carpenter. Married dressmaker Edith Hand on 5 December 1912. Died in Christchurch on 19 November 1964.

10. **Arnold Wallis (1885–1956).** Born in Christchurch on 14 February 1885. Never married. Died on 25 November 1956.

11. **Winifred Olive Owen (née Wallis) (1888–1964).** Born in Christchurch on 23 March 1888. Married Donald Owen on 7 September 1914 who abandoned her in Wellington. Died in Christchurch on 18 August 1964.

12. **Wilfred Stanley Wallis (1891–1957).** Born in Ōpāwa, Christchurch on 15 May 1891. He was an orthopaedic surgeon, hospital superintendent and artist. Married Elsie Ada Williams at Timaru on 18 May 1915. Served with the Medical Corps during World War I. Died in Rotorua on 20 September 1957.

The family home of Eliza and John Wallis at 49 Ensors Road, Ōpāwa, Christchurch. This is where many of their children would have been born.

The Sweating System
New Zealand Observer and Free Lance, 1888

In the late 1880s and early 1890 several of Eliza's daughters were employed as dressmakers, tailoresses, and machinists. At that time much of this work was 'sweated labour' with women working long hours in often poor conditions for little pay or in their own homes via the piecework system, where they were paid for each piece made, rather than by the hour.

The sweating scandal exposed these working conditions to the public, and the Dunedin Tailoresses' Union was created on 12 July 1889, the first women's trade union in New Zealand. This was followed by the Christchurch Tailoresses and Pressers Union and the Auckland Tailoresses Union amongst others who joined together as the New Zealand Federated Tailoresses' Unions, holding their first conference in Christchurch in July 1891. Members of the unions also worked for women's suffrage.

The unions threatened employers with strike action as they worked to raise wages and establish industry standards for tailoresses. This led to investigations into the conditions of women's work in other trades as well.

NEW ZEALAND TIMELINE

Edward and Sarah Hart (née Culley)

1802 (October 26): Edward Hart's father is suffering from famishing (starvation) and receives a payment from the Thurnham Parish Overseer.

1804 (October): Edward's father dies just before Edward turns two years old. Edward's widowed mother receives regular payments from Parish Overseers.

1823 (August 24): Edward marries Sarah Culley in St Mary's church at Thurnham.

1823 (September 5): First child, Sarah, baptised the month after their marriage.

1824: Edward in Kent Gaol for 'destroying rabbits'. His mother remarries to Richard Battam on 24 December.

1825 (February 2): Sarah pregnant with their second child when Edward burgles William Akehurst's home and goes 'on the run'.

1825 (April 17): Second child, Edward, baptised.

1825 (December 14): London bank Pole and Co. fail, sparking 40 other bank failures and an 80 per cent drop in the London stock market.

1827 (July 2): 17 months after the burglary, Edward is caught.

1827 (August 16): Edward is sentenced to seven years transportation.

1827 (September 1): Edward is sent to *The Retribution*, a prison hulk moored on the River Medway near Sheerness.

1830 (December 24): Former soldier John Dyke is tried, convicted and publicly hanged on Penenden Heath in Maidstone for setting fire to a farm in Bearsted during the 'Swing Riots' as agricultural workers riot over lack of work. Dyke says of Edward, 'Hart was a good-hearted fellow'.[1]

1833 (July 1): Edward is given a free pardon after serving six years on prison hulks in England and Bermuda.

1834 (October 26): Third child, William, baptised.

1834 (February): Sarah's mother, Margaret Culley (née Corne), dies.

1834 (October 4): Third child, William, dies and is buried in Thurnham.

1835 (October 1835): Declaration of the Independence of New Zealand signed by the United Tribes of New Zealand.

1837 (January 30): Hart family move to Maidstone in Kent. Fourth child, Ellen, born.

1840 (February 6): Treaty of Waitangi signed by Māori women as well as men. A sub-colony of the Colony of New South Wales, the following year New Zealand was established as a Crown colony in its own right, the Colony of New Zealand, and reported to London instead of Sydney.

1841 (April 9): The Hart family appear on the *Register of Emigrant Labourers who have received a Free Passage to New Zealand*, boarding The New Zealand Company sailing ship *Tyne* at the port of Gravesend in Kent. Edward is Emigrants' Cook during the voyage. Also on board are Sir William Martin (first Chief Justice of New Zealand), William Swainson (second Attorney-General of New Zealand) and Thomas Outhwaite (register of the Supreme Court) who during their four months at sea draft laws which in December see the Supreme Court of New Zealand established.

1841 (August 9): The 500 ton barque *Tyne* arrives at Port Nicholson (Wellington) but anchors off Kaiwarra. There is no wharf at Port Nicholson so a basket lowers passengers into a boat and then sailors carry them ashore. The Hart family are said to have lived in the school house until a mud hut was built in Hick's Paddock above the beach.

1846 (March 30): Fourth child, Eliza, born in Wellington [birth unregistered].

1847: Sixth child, Rose, born in Wellington [birth unregistered].

John and Eliza Wallis (née Hart)

1852: New Zealand Constitution Act passes limiting the franchise to males 21 and over, not serving a criminal sentence and with European title to land. New Zealand is now a self-governing colony.

1853 (July 4–October 1): First New Zealand General Election — Eliza seven years old. Her father, Edward, is registered to vote.

1854 (May): Eliza's maternal grandfather, William Culley, dies in the Hollingbourne Union Workhouse near Maidstone, at the age of 93.

1855 (October 28–December 28): Second New Zealand General Election — Eliza nine years old. Her paternal grandmother, Margaret Battam (née Siphlet), dies in Maidstone.

1860/1861 (December 12–March 28): Third New Zealand General Election — Eliza almost 15 years old.

1863 (January 13): Sixteen-year-old Eliza marries John Wallis in Wellington. Still a minor, her father Edward gives his consent and signs his name as a witness with an X.

1863 (August 23): First child, Emily, born in Wellington.

1865: Second child, Herbert, born and dies in Wellington.

1866 (February 12–April 6): Fourth New Zealand General Election — Eliza 20 years old.

1867: Third child, John, born in Wellington.

1868: Third child, John, dies in Wellington.

1869 (June): John Stuart Mill publishes 'The Subjection of Women' in Britain, his 'perfect equality' essay which influences New Zealand feminists.

1869 (August 18): Mary Ann Müller (née Wilson) writing as *Fémmina*, publishes 'An appeal to the men of New Zealand', writing 'Our women are brave and strong, with an amount of self-reliance and freedom from conventionalities eminently calculated to form a great nation. Give them scope' and 'The change is coming, but why is New Zealand only to follow? Why not take the initiative?'

1869 (November 24): Fourth child, Frederick Arthur, born in Wellington.

1871 (January 14–February 23): Fifth New Zealand General Election — Eliza almost 25 years old. Feminist and social reformer Mary Ann Colclough (née Barnes), writing for various colonial newspapers as 'Polly Plum', argues that women should not be subject to legislation they had no part in making.

1872: Fifth child, Alice Matilda, born in Wellington.

c.1873: Wallis family move to Christchurch.

1874: Sixth child, Gertrude May, born in Christchurch. John Chapman Andrew urges the House of Representatives to enfranchise women.

1875: Abolition of provinces. The new local government organisation gives same electoral right to women ratepayers as men.

1875/1876 (December 30–March 28): Sixth New Zealand General Election — Eliza almost 29 years old.

1877 (January 22): Seventh child Elizabeth ('Edith') born in Christchurch. Education Act means women can stand and vote for Education Boards.

1877 (July 11): Kate Edger graduates with a BA in Latin and Mathematics from the University of New Zealand, the first woman to gain a university degree and the first woman in the British Empire to earn a BA.

1878: Robert Stout's Electoral Bill that women ratepayers be eligible to vote for, and be elected as, members of the House of Representatives, is unsuccessful.

1879 (Long Economic Depression): Unemployment grows along with social misery and unrest. Women and children are exploited and evidence emerges of sweated labour and poor working conditions in several industries.

1879 (April 26): Eighth child, Ellen Sarah, born in Christchurch.

1879 (August 28–September 15): Seventh New Zealand General Election — Eliza 32 years old.

1879 (October 8): John and Eliza's daughter Emily gives birth to an illegitimate daughter, Esther, who Eliza will raise until aged 10.

1880: Women's Franchise Bill introduced by James Wallis lapses after first reading.

1880 (March 12): Eliza's mother Sarah dies in Wellington, aged 74.

1881 (December 9): Eighth New Zealand General Election — Eliza 34 years old. Women are eligible as electors or representatives of licensing committees. Terms of Employment of Females and other Acts set minimum age of woman workers at 12 and overtime rate for woman workers under 18. Another Women's Franchise Bill introduced by James Wallis withdrawn before its second reading. New Zealander Helen Connon is the first woman in the British Empire to win a degree with honours.

1882 (February 13): Ninth child, Frank Leonard, born in Christchurch.

1884 (June 22): Ninth New Zealand General Election — Eliza 38 years old.

1884 (November 23): Eliza's father, Edward, dies in Wellington, aged 82. The Married Women's Property Act recognises married women's legal existence and restores to them the right to acquire, hold and dispose of any land or property.

1885 (February 14): Tenth child, Arnold, born in Christchurch.

1885: Women win the right to vote on hospital boards and charitable aid board elections. Eliza becomes a founding member of the New Zealand Women's Christian Temperance Union (WCTU) which was established following the visit of American temperance campaigner Mary Leavitt.

The Women's Suffrage Movement

1886 (February 23): First annual meeting of the WCTU held in Wellington where they resolve to work for women's suffrage.

1887 (September 26): 10th New Zealand General Election — Eliza 41 years old.

1887: Two petitions requesting the franchise are signed by around 350 women and presented to the House of Representatives.

1888 (March 23): Eleventh child, Winifred Olive, born in Christchurch. Two petitions requesting the enfranchisement of women are signed by around 800 women and presented to the Legislative Council.

1889: Tailoresses' Union of New Zealand founded.

1890 (April 22): Eliza's granddaughter is adopted by Minnie Dean at Winton (Esther Wallis Dean). 'In 1890, with Charles's consent, she [Minnie] adopted Esther Wallis to assist with looking after the children'.[2]

1890 (August 5): Sir John Hall proposes franchise extended to women, the motion passes. Women's Franchise Bill introduced on 19 August, but defeated on 21 August.

1890 (December 5): Eleventh New Zealand General Election — Eliza 44 years old.

1891 (May 15): Twelfth child, Wilfred Stanley, born in Opawa, Christchurch.

1891 (August 24): Eight suffrage petitions signed by more than 9,000 women are presented to the House of Representatives. A Woman's Suffrage Bill introduced by Sir John Hall receives majority support in the House of Representatives but is narrowly defeated in the Legislative Council.

1892: Minnie registers Esther Wallis Dean at Winton School. Eliza is a founding member of the Canterbury Women's Institute (CWI), which would spearhead the suffrage campaign in Canterbury. The Women's Franchise League is established and six petitions asking for the vote, with more than 17,000 signatures, are presented to the House of Representatives. Eliza and her daughter Emily have signed Sheet 234 (names 419 and 418).

1893: Eliza is part of The Society for the Protection of Women and Children (SPWC) formed to 'prosecute in cases of cruelty, seduction, outrage or excessive violence to women and children', give advice and aid to women who had been cruelly treated, provide neglected children with homes, and lobby for improvements in the law with respect to women and children.

1893 (June): Electoral Bill introduced by Richard Seddon. During debate there is majority support for the enfranchisement of Māori as well as Pākehā women. Women's Franchise Bill passes Lower House on 8 July.

1893 (July 28): The 'monster petition' of Mary Jane Carpenter (nee Griffiths) and 25,521 others (including Eliza and Emily Wallis) is submitted to Parliament, along with several other petitions: Kate Baldwin (+2,765), Gerald Loftus Torin Peacocke (+2,301 male supporters), Elizabeth Milne Gregory Eyre-Kenny (nee Buchanan) (+601), Caroline Anderson (+393), Johanna Wilson (nee Munro) (+83), Marian Kirker (+49), Clara Maud Birch (later Burrows) (+40), Sophia James (+34), Lizzie Frost Rattray (nee Fenton) (+31), Harriet Win (nee Humphreys) (+23), F Nightingale (+16) and Sarah Lurchin (+15).

1893 (August 11): Sir John Hall presents the Women's Suffrage Petitions to the House of Representatives.

1893 (September 8): Women's Franchise Bill passes the Upper House (Legislative Council), allowing enfranchisement of women. Evenly divided Council members have seen Richard Seddon telegraphing Thomas Kelly, a Liberal Party councillor, to change his vote from in favour of the bill to against it. Two other councillors, William Reynold and Edward Stevens, are furious at Seddon's manipulation and change their votes, allowing the bill to pass 20 votes to 18. Seddon's meddling has backfired.

1893 (September 19): New Zealand Governor, David Boyle Glasgow, signs into law the Electoral Act that gives all women in New Zealand the right to vote. He was petitioned by 18 legislative councillors to withhold his consent but suffragists responded by showering him with telegrams and requests to receive deputations. All women in New Zealand aged 21 or over now have the right to vote.

1893 (September 22): Women in the Cook Islands are allowed to participate in elections for island councils and a federal parliament. They go to the polls on 14 October.

1893 (November 28): Twelfth New Zealand General Election — Eliza 47 years old. 85 per cent of all those eligible, a total of 109,461 women, have registered to vote. 90,290 women cast their votes. The following day Elizabeth Yates (née Oman) is elected Mayor of the borough of Onehunga, the first woman in the British Empire to hold such an office.

1893 (December 20): First vote by Māori women as elections are held in the Māori electorates. The total number on the Māori roll is 11,269, which includes around 4,000 women.

1895 (May): First issue of the WCTU's newspaper *The White Ribbon* is issued. The first New Zealand newspaper to be owned and operated solely by women and contains articles on the latest ideas in health, childcare, divorcee rights, nutrition, dress, ex-prisoner's rights, and equality within the marriage. Eliza worked on the publication and an article about the WCTU convention of 1899 lists her as 'Mrs Wallis (White Ribbon paper)'.

1895 (May 9 and 11): Minnie and Charles Dean arrested. 'When Dean was arrested she had six children in her care, including Esther. All were content and healthy, if poorly dressed and living in squalor'.[3] 'Esther Wallis and Margaret Cameron, who had left 'The Larches' to live a life of her own, looked after the children when Mrs Dean was arrested, until the police placed them in a Charitable Aid Board in Invercargill'.[4]

1895 (May 11): Nineteen-year-old Margaret and fifteen-year-old Esther are called upon to identify the bodies recovered from 'The Larches': 'Both girls had been present at the exhumation of the bodies and, despite the grisly nature of the scene, had obviously treated the tiny corpses to close inspection. They both considered the skull of the older child (now with only a piece of the scalp and hair attached) to be that of an adoptive brother named Willie Phelan. Under questioning, Margaret Cameron recalled the details of a number of other children whose whereabouts had not yet been established'.[5]

1895 (June 8): Charles Dean is discharged without conviction and likely attempted to frighten Esther and influence her testimony: 'That their adopted father's presence or absence at the coronial hearings may have had some bearing on the nature of the girls' testimony is evidenced by an aside included in the newspaper report on the third inquest. Both the Press and the Hawkes Bay Herald reported a complaint by Sergeant MacDonnell that after his release Charles Dean, despite being "warned not to do so", had "forced himself" into the Charitable Aid Board home where Esther Wallace [Wallis] was being boarded. After having managed to "communicate" with his adopted daughter, Sergeant MacDonnell claimed that "the girl was not now so willing to give evidence as she had been". While the nature of this exchange is not clear, it is possible that Charles attempted to intimidate or dissuade Esther from testifying honestly'.[6]

1895 (June 18): Minnie Dean's Supreme Court trial begins in Invercargill. Margaret and Esther are called to give evidence: 'Another child, Willie Phelp, Mrs. Dean brought from Dunedin five years ago. He was then about two years. The child remained at Larches a few months after September, 1893, and disappeared when no one was about the house but Mrs. Dean, who said a woman from Invercargill came for him. Mrs. Dean did not treat this child well. She would knock him down and seize him by the hair and bump his head on the floor. Mrs. Dean was in the habit of getting drunk, but was always sober when she abused the child. Some children she treated well, others not so well. She used to get drunk by herself. Cyril Scoular was about four years old when he disappeared. Esther Wallace [Wallis] corroborated Cameron's evidence re the disappearance of the children, and said she was sent out of the way on all occasions. Mrs. Dean made her take the children with her, and only the one that disappeared was left behind in the house on each occasion. From the hair, she thought the skeleton was Willie Phelan, whose new velvet suit was in the house after he disappeared'.[7]

1895 (June 21): Minnie Dean found guilty of infanticide.

1895 (August 12): Minnie Dean hanged at Invercargill Prison, the first and only New Zealand woman to receive the death penalty. She was buried in Winton Cemetery.

1896 (April 13–18): The Canterbury Women's Institute send out invitations to the women of New Zealand to attend a convention at the Provincial Council Chambers in Christchurch. Delegates from eleven women's groups from throughout the country attend and together they form the National Council of Women (NCWNZ). Eliza is a founding member. Topics in the first four years included marriage, divorce and the economic independence of women, parental responsibilities and equal pay for equal work. They protested unequal laws relating to men and women, including women's inability to become members of Parliament or to hold other public offices. Dr Emily Siedeberg-McKinnon studied medicine at the University of Otago from 1891 to 1895, graduating in 1896 as the first woman to gain a medical degree in New Zealand.

1896 (December 4): Thirteenth New Zealand General Election — Eliza 50 years old.

1897: Ethel Benjamin is the first woman lawyer in New Zealand.

1899 (December 6): Fourteenth New Zealand General Election — Eliza 53 years old.

1902 (November 25): Fifteenth New Zealand General Election — Eliza 56 years old.

1903 (May 27): John Wallis dies, aged 64, from the autoimmune disease *pernicious anemia*, caused by a person's inability to absorb vitamin B12. He was buried in Linwood Cemetery on 31 May 1903.

1903: Eliza receives a postcard from fellow suffragist Kate Sheppard, who is two years younger than her. Because of the content it is believed to have been sent sometime after John's death in May. See page 22.

1905 (December 6): Sixteenth New Zealand General Election — Eliza 59 years old.

1907 (September 26): The United Kingdom grants 'Dominion' status in the British Empire to New Zealand, now known as the *Dominion of New Zealand*.

1908 (November 17–December 1): Seventeenth New Zealand General Election — Eliza 62 years old.

1911 (December 7–14): Eighteenth New Zealand General Election — Eliza 65 years old.

1914 (September 15): Eliza dies at her home, 179 Ensors Road in Linwood, Christchurch at the age of 68. Her cause of death is peritoneal cancer, a rare form of cancer. Eliza was buried with John in Linwood Cemetery on 17 September (Block 33 Plot 234).

1919 (October 29): The Women's Parliamentary Rights Act gives women the right to stand for election to the House of Representatives.

1923: Ellen Melville first woman to run as candidate in a Parliamentary election.

1933: Elizabeth McCombs becomes the first woman Member of Parliament (MP), winning a by-election in the Lyttelton seat. Legal marriage age raised from 12 to 14.

1938: A law passes allowing women to join police force.

1941: First ten policewomen appointed, but are not allowed outside duties until 1947. Women gain the right to sit in the Legislative Council, the nominated Upper House of Parliament.

1946: Mary Dreaver and Mary Patricia Anderson are the first women appointed to the Legislative Council.

1947: Mabel Howard becomes the first woman Pākehā Cabinet minister.

1949: Iriaka Rātana becomes the first woman Māori MP. Her husband, Matiu, member for the Western Māori electorate, was killed in a car accident. Iriaka, heavily pregnant, looking after 6 children, and running the family farm, stood for his seat. She was elected by a sweeping majority.

1951 (September): Te Ropu Wahine Māori Toko i te Ora (Māori Women's Welfare League) formed in Wellington.

1953: First Family Planning Clinic opens Remuera. Ethel McMillan elected to Parliament (Dunedin North). She would become longest serving woman MP (22 years).

1966: Te Ata-i-Rangikaahu chosen as Maori Queen (sixth monarch).

1969 (August 22): Voting age lowered from 21 to 20.

1970: Whetu Tirikatene-Sullivan is the first woman to give birth while an MP.

Mabel Howard

1972: Whetu Tirikātene-Sullivan (Ngāi Tahu, Ngāti Kahungunu) becomes first woman Māori Cabinet minister. Women chain themselves to Christchurch Cathedral's iron railings to commemorate Suffrage Day by protesting at the condition of women.

1973: Domestic Purposes Benefit introduced. United Women's Convention (Auckland).

1974: First Women's Refuge set up in Christchurch. Voting age lowered from 20 to 18.

1981: Sonja Davies first woman Vice-President of the Federation of Labour.

1983: The Letters Patent declare New Zealand the 'Realm of New Zealand'. MP Ruth Richardson pushes to be able to breastfeed her baby at work.

1984: Ann Hercus is the first Minister for Women's Affairs.

1986: The Constitution Act 1986 removes the residual power of the United Kingdom Parliament to legislate for New Zealand at its request and consent. The Act lays down the framework defining fundamental political principles of governance and establishes the powers of the executive, legislative and judicial branches of state.

Iriaka Rātana

1987: Nadja Tollemache appointed first woman Ombudsman.

1989: Sylvia Cartwright elected first woman chief district court judge. Helen Clark first woman Deputy Prime Minister.

1990: Catherine Tizard appointed first woman Governor-General (Te Kāwana Tianara o Aotearoa). Kate Sheppard's likeness replaces that of Queen Elizabeth II on the front of the New Zealand $10 note (fifth issue).

1993: In 1991 the New Zealand government establishes a '1993 Suffrage Centennial Trust'. The trust uses $5 million (over 3 years) for various projects celebrating Māori and Pākehā women's achievements. The New Zealand Suffrage Centennial Medal 1993 (authorised by the Queen) is awarded to 546 selected people, honouring their contribution and work in campaigning for women's suffrage or another issue of women's rights in New Zealand, or both.

1997: Jennifer Mary Shipley (née Robson) becomes first woman Prime Minister (Te Pirimia o Aotearoa) after Jim Bolger resigns as leader of the National Party.

1999: Labour's Helen Clark becomes New Zealand's first elected woman Prime Minister following the General Election of November 1999. Clark would be PM for nine years, becoming New Zealand's fifth-longest-serving PM.

2002: MP Katherine Rich feeds her baby in the debating chamber. While giving a speech a fellow female MP shouted, 'Go home to your kids'.

2005: Margaret Wilson elected first woman Speaker of the House of Representatives.

2016: Patricia Lee Reddy [Patsy] is appointed twenty-first Governor-General.

2017: Jacinda Kate Laurell Ardern becomes the world's youngest woman leader when elected fortieth Prime Minister at age 37.

2018: Suffrage 125 events are coordinated by the Ministry for Women, Te Minitatanga mō ngā Wāhine.

2018 (February 5): Jacinda Ardern becomes the first woman Prime Minister given the right to speak during formal proceedings at Waitangi.

2018 (June 21): Jacinda Ardern is the first Prime Minister to have a baby while in office, and the world's second elected head of government to give birth while in office.

Rt Hon Helen Clark

Jacinda Adern

Dame Catherine Tizard

Dame Jenny Shipley

ENDNOTES

1. *Maidstone Journal* (30 November 1830).
2. Rawle, J. (1997). *Minnie Dean: A Hundred Years of Memory*. Christchurch New Zealand: Orca Publishing (p. 9).
3. Sell, Bronwyn (2009). *Law Breakers and Mischief Makers: 50 Notorious New Zealanders* (p. 68).
4. Rawle, J. (1997). *Minnie Dean: A Hundred Years of Memory*. Christchurch New Zealand: Orca Publishing (p. 20).
5. Powell, Debra (2013). *The Ogress, the Innocent, and the Madman: Narrative and Gender in Child Homicide Trials in New Zealand, 1870-1925* [Thesis, University of Waikato] (p. 312).
6. 'The Winton Baby Farming Case', *Press* (Canterbury) 11 June 1895, p. 5 / 'The Winton Baby Farmer', *Hawkes Bay Herald*, 11 June 1895, p. 4. As quoted in Powell, Debra (2013). *The Ogress, the Innocent, and the Madman: Narrative and Gender in Child Homicide Trials in New Zealand, 1870-1925* [Thesis, University of Waikato] (p. 312).
7. *New Zealand Herald* (11 June 1895). The Winton Baby Farming Cases.

WORLD SUFFRAGE TIMELINE

1755 Corsican Republic (revoked by the French in 1769)

1756 In Massachusetts Lydia Taft casts a ballot in place of her deceased husband (lost 1780)

1776 United States Declaration of Independence signed: New Hampshire (lost 1784), New Jersey (propertied women, expanded 1790, lost 1807), New York (lost 1777).

1792 Sierra Leone (lost 1808, full 1930)

1838 Pitcairn Islands (ruling councils)

1856 Norfolk Island (after 194 residents of Pitcairn moved here)

1869 Wyoming Territory US (confirmed statehood 1890)

1870 Utah Territory US (until 1887, reinstated 1895)

1881 Isle of Man (propertied women, full 1919)

1883 Washington Territory US (declared unconstitutional in 1887)

1887 Montana Territory US

1889 Franceville (French Pacific colony until renamed New Hebrides)

1893 New Zealand (self-governing British colony)

1893 Cook Islands (island councils and a federal parliament)

1893 Colorado State US

1894 Colony of South Australia

1896 Idaho State US

1899 Colony of Western Australia

1902 Australia (Aborigines 1962)

1906 Finland (Grand Duchy of the Russian Empire until 1917)

1908 Denmark (limited, full 1915), Faroe Islands (limited, full 1915), Greenland (limited, full 1915), Iceland (local — women over 40, national 1915, full 1920)

1910 Washington State US

1911 California US, Portugal (limited, then illegal, restricted 1931, full 1976)

1912 Arizona, Kansas, Oregon - US

1913 Alaska US, Illinois US (limited), Norway

1914 Montana US, Nevada US

1916 Alberta, Manitoba, Saskatchewan - Canada

1917 Arkansas US, Armenia (Russia 1917, full 1919), British Columbia (Canada), Canada (limited, Indigenous Canadians 1960), Estonia, Indiana US, Latvia, Lithuania, Michigan US, Nebraska US, Netherlands (limited, full 1919), New York US, North Dakota US (presidential suffrage), Ohio US (lost later that year), Ontario (Canada), Rhode Island US, Russia/Soviet Union, Uruguay

1918 Austria, Azerbaijan, Czechoslovakia, Georgia, Germany, Hungary (full 1945), Jersey (partial, full 1945), Kyrgyzstan, Lithuania, Nova Scotia (Canada), Oklahoma US, Poland, South Dakota US, Ireland (women over 30, full 1922) United Kingdom (women over 30, full 1928), Russia

1919 Belarus, Belgium (partial, full 1948), Luxembourg, New Brunswick (limited, Canada), Sweden, Ukraine, Zimbabwe (formerly Southern Rhodesia, full 1980),

1920 Albania, Czech Republic (formerly Czechoslovakia), Slovakia (formerly Czechoslovakia), United States (19th Amendment, women can vote in both state and federal elections, full 1965)

1921 Prince Edward Island (Canada), Mumbai, India (formerly Bombay), Chennai, India (formerly Madras)

1922 Myanmar (formerly Burma)

1924 Kazakhstan, Mongolia, St Lucia, Tajikistan, Turkmen

1925 Italy (full 1945)

1925 Newfoundland (Canada), Trinidad & Tobago (women over 30, full 1945)

1927 Turkmenistan

1929 Ecuador (full 1967), Moldova (full 1940), Puerto Rico (full 1935)

1930 Greece (full 1952), South Africa (restricted, Black South Africans 1994)

1931 Spain (until 1936, full 1976), Sri Lanka (formerly Ceylon)

1932 Brazil, Maldives, Thailand

1934 Chile (restricted, full 1949), Cuba, Turkey

1935 India (limited, full 1947)

1936 Virgin Islands (restricted, full 1951)

1937 Bulgaria (full 1944), Indonesia (full 1945), Philippines

1938 Bolivia (full 1952), Romania (restricted, full 1946), Uzbekistan

1938 El Salvador (partial 1950, full 1961)

1940 Quebec (Canada)

1941 Panama (full 1946)

1942 Dominican Republic

1944 Bermuda, France, Jamaica

1945 Guatemala (full 1965), Senegal, Togo, Yugoslavia (now Serbia, Montenegro, Croatia, Slovenia, Bosnia & Herzegovina, Macedonia)

1946 Cameroon, Djibouti, Guatemala, North Korea (one-party state), Liberia (limited), Macedonia, Venezuela, Vietnam (one-party state)

1947 Argentina, China, Japan, Malta, Mexico, Pakistan, Singapore, Taiwan

1948 Israel, Niger, Seychelles, South Korea, Suriname

1949 Bosnia & Herzegovina, Costa Rica, Hong Kong, Netherlands Antilles, Syria (limited, full 1953)

1950 Barbados, Haiti

1951 Antigua & Barbuda, Dominica, Grenada, Montserrat, Nepal (suspended 1960 & 2005, full 2008), St Christopher (Kitts) & Nevis, St Lucia, St Vincent & the Grenadines

1952 Cote d'Ivoire, Lebanon

1953 Bhutan, Guyana,

1954 Belize, Colombia, Ghana

1955 Cambodia, Eritrea, Ethiopia, Honduras, Nicaragua, Peru

1956 Benin, Comoros, Egypt, Gabon, Mali, Mauritius, Somalia

1957 Malaysia, Tunisia

1958 Burkina Faso, Chad, Guinea, Laos, Nigeria (full 1976)

1959 Brunei (since suspended), Madagascar, San Marino, Tanzania

1960 Cyprus, Gambia, Tonga

1961 Bahamas, Burundi, Malawi, Mauritania, Paraguay, Rwanda

1962 Algeria, Monaco, Uganda, Zambia (Northern Rhodesia)

1963 Congo Republic, Equatorial Guinea, Fiji, Iran, Kenya, Morocco

1964 Libya, Papua New Guinea, Sudan

1965 Afghanistan, Botswana, Lesotho

1967 Democratic Republic of the Congo, Kiribati, Tuvalu, Yemen, Zaire

1968 Nauru, Swaziland

1970 Andora

1971 Switzerland

1972 Bangladesh

1974 Jordan, Solomon Islands

1975 Angola, Cape Verde, Mozambique, São Tomé & Principe, Vanuatu

1976 East Timor (Timor-Leste)

1977 Guinea-Bissau

1979 Marshall Islands, Fed States of Micronesia, Palau

1980 Iraq

1984 Liechtenstein

1985 Kuwait (removed 1999, re-granted 2005)

1986 Central African Republic

1989 Namibia

1990 Samoa

1996 Palestine (elections delayed since 2006)

1997 Oman (full 2002)

1999 Qatar (elections delayed)

2002 Bahrain

2006 United Arab Emirates (limited)

2015 Saudi Arabia (municipal elections)

Note

Brunei: citizens denied the right to vote or to stand for election since 1962.

Vatican City: The only people with voting rights are cardinals (and the only voting is for a new Pope). As only men can become cardinals, woman have no say in the election of a new Pope.

Eliza & the white camellia activities

Create & make

Knitted suffragist camellia

You will need yarn in gold, white and violet. The size of your camellia will depend upon your needle size (I use 3.5mm) and the thickness of your yarn.

Violet yarn: cast on 120 stitches.

Rows 1-4: Knit

Row 5: Knit 3 stitches together across the row (40 stitches)

Rows 6-9: Knit

Row 10: Knit 2 stitches together across the row (20 stitches)

Rows 11-14: Knit

Row 15: Knit 2 stitches together across the row (10 stitches)

Cut yarn, leaving a 20cm tail.

Thread the tail onto a tapestry needle and slip the 10 remaining stitches onto the needle then pull tight.

Pull the camellia into a circle, then stitch up the seam and sew in the ends.

White yarn: cast on 120 stitches.

Rows 1-2: Knit

Row 3: Knit 3 stitches together across the row (40 stitches)

Rows 4-5: Knit

Row 6: Knit 2 stitches together across the row (20 stitches)

Rows 7-8: Knit

Row 9: Knit 2 stitches together across the row (10 stitches)

Cut yarn, leaving a 20cm tail and stitch together as above.

Gold yarn: cast on 16 stitches.

Cast off. Coil into a tight spiral. Stack the violet and yellow flowers together then sew the gold spiral into the middle to represent the stamens.

Alternatively use a gold button with 4 holes and sew to the centre of the camellia.

Sew a safety pin onto the back of the camellia so you can attach it to your clothing or suffragist sash.

Paper plate suffragist camellia

Take four paper plates.

- Cut flower petal shapes about 6cm deep around the outside of one plate.
- Cut 2cm off the rim of the next paper plate, then cut the same petal shape.
- Cut 4cm off the rim of the next paper plate, then cut the same petal shape.
- Cut 6cm off the outside of the next paper plate, then cut the same petal shape.
- Curl all the 'petals' upwards around a pen and into a flower shape.
- Staple or glue the plates together largest to smallest and use a yellow felt pen or small round stickers to create the stamens of the camellia.

Suffragist rosette

Draw and cut out four circular templates on paper, 8cm, 6cm, 5cm and 3cm in diameter. You can mix and match your fabrics, but this is what we used:

- Cut two circles out of violet felt: 8cm and 5cm diameter
- Cut one circle out of white fabric: 6cm diameter
- Cut one circle out of gold fabric: 5cm diameter
- Cut three ribbons in suffrage colours, gold, white and violet: 15cm long
- Front: Stack the circles (apart from the 5cm violet felt one) on top of each other from largest to smallest. Pin together. Place a button in the middle of the smallest circle and sew on, fastening the layers together.

- Back: Fasten the ribbons together at one end with a couple of stitches. On the reverse of the large felt circle, place the stitched end of the ribbons in the middle and cover with the 5cm violet felt circle on top so that they hang down together. Hand sew the small circle to the large one, making sure the ribbons are securely attached. Cut an upwards facing triangle out of the ends of each ribbon. Sew a safety pin in the middle of the small felt circle. This will be used to pin the rosette to your clothing.

Make a suffragist hat

Find an old hat and convert it to show your support for the suffragist cause. Sew or glue onto the hat some or all of the following:

- ribbons in gold, white or violet
- artificial white 'camellia' flowers
- rosettes or knitted flowers you have made
- a piece of white card with 'Votes for Women' on it.

Paper suffragist sash

- Cut two 11cm wide strips of newsprint or kraft paper 900cm long.
- Cut 3.5cm strips of crepe paper in the suffrage colours gold, white and violet.

  - Glue the strips onto both lengths of the paper.
  - Once dry, put the right sides of the paper strips together matching the colours.
  - Measure 5cm down from the top on the gold side and mark, then using a ruler draw a line from the mark on an angle up to the corner where the purple colour is. Staple along this line with 5 staples to join both sides and trim the excess off with scissors.
  - At the opposite bottom end of the strips fold each end up 45° with the gold strip having the shortest length, then trim.
  - Place the sash over your left shoulder and fasten ends together over your right hip using a stapler or brooch.
  - Alternatively you can rule lines on the newsprint and use crayons or paint to colour in your suffrage colours.
- If you want to, you can letter a suffrage slogan on the white stripe of your sash, such as 'Votes for Women'.

Suffragist bunting

Paper bunting:

- Cut a length of 45cm wide paper as long as you wish.
- Fold the 45cm width in half, so it now measures 22.5 wide.
- Cut triangles out of the paper, don't be too worried about measuring as they will all end up roughly equal due to the folded paper.
- Decorate using the colours gold, white and violet, or with suffrage slogans or pictures.
- Staple the bunting onto string, yarn or ribbon.

Fabric bunting:

- Draw a triangle on cardboard and cut it out to use as a bunting template.
- Pin the template to gold, white or violet fabric and cut around it using pinking shears to cut a zigzag edge in the fabric which stops it fraying. Repeat until you have enough flags for your desired bunting length.
- Evenly space the flags along 1.3cm-wide bias binding tape, leaving 40cm of tape free at each end for hanging your bunting. Fold the shortest fabric edge over the tape, and pin it in place.
- Sew the flags onto the bias binding, either hand-stitching with a needle and thread or with a sewing machine.

Classroom activities

Action: Organise a petition

Choose a topic or issue and organise a petition about it.

- Gather signatures and hold meetings to discuss the issue.
- Hold a march around your school with placards, or in 1890s costumes on bicycles.
- Present the petition to your teacher, parents or school principal.

Campaigning: Hold an election

Form political parties with your classmates and discuss how you will run your campaign.

- Give speeches and let your classmates know what your party stands for.
- Hold an election and see which political party wins.

Debate: Why should men have the vote?

Prepare two groups to debate the issue: Why should men have the vote?

Allow time to research the topic and hold the debate in front of an audience.

Here is a scenario to get students thinking:

'Welcome to 1893 and the new herstory. Society is dominated by women, who have been voting since New Zealand's first General Election was held in 1853. They are fully engaged in work, society and political life. Men are the primary homemakers and responsible for rearing children...after the women have given birth. Now men have decided they want a say in governing the country, too. They are holding meetings and gathering signatures on a suffrage petition to present to parliament. The debate rages as to whether it would do the country any good whatsoever for men to be granted the vote, with many viewing it as an attack on natural gender roles that could lead to the breakdown of society. A few women support the men in their endeavours, but social commentators are saying things like:

- Tampering with men's and women's 'natural' gender roles could cause the breakdown of society – or at least screaming babies, burnt dinners and cats in the milk jug.
- Women have the vote and the power at the present moment; I say for Heaven's sake let us keep it!
- There are obvious disadvantages about having men in Parliament. I do not know what is going to be done about their top hats. How are we to see if they are sitting in front of us?'

Design: Women's suffrage medal

In 1993 the New Zealand Government created a women's suffrage medal to commemorate 100 years since women were granted the vote. Design your own medal and make a gold, white and violet ribbon to hang it on.

Design: Women's suffrage poster

Design and create a poster on one of the following:

- History of women's suffrage including a timeline
- Display poster for suffrage
- Women's traditional roles
- Rational dress
- The introduction of the 'modern' bicycle in the 1890s and what this meant for women.

Discuss: Stereotypes

Look at stereotypes of women and men in 19th Century New Zealand.

- Discuss in the classroom how this affected why women didn't get the vote until 1893.
- How are women treated in other countries?
- How did women's roles change during World War I (1914–1918) and how did this affect overseas women being granted the vote?

Explore: Women's suffrage worldwide

Although New Zealand women were granted the vote in 1893, many women in other countries didn't get the vote until much later.

- Explore women's rights around the world.
- Write 500 words about when suffrage was achieved in another country. See the World Suffrage Timeline on page 33.
- Research women's voting experience in one of the following places: Afghanistan, Egypt, Kenya, Nigeria, Oman, Pakistan, Papa New Guinea, Qatar, Saudi Arabia, Uganda or Zanzibar.

Group activity: Voting

The class separates into two groups.

- Students are told they can watch a movie or sport and in their groups will discuss how to vote as to which movie or sport to watch.
- Before they actually vote, one group is told that they are not allowed to vote, that the other group will decide.
- The voting group decide which movie to watch or which sport to watch.
- The groups come together and the teacher asks how one group of students felt about being excluded from the decision?

- Also discuss if that is fair or not and if it is a good idea to exclude some people when the outcome of the vote will affect everyone.
- The discussion then moves onto the 1890s when women felt excluded from making decisions about issues that affected them.
- Repeat the activity, allowing everyone to vote. Discuss how women felt when they had the vote and could affect the outcome of elections.

Inquiry: Campaigning

Students identify a present-day women's rights issue such as equal pay.

- Prepare a campaign that supports this issue.
- Make campaign material which could include placards for a peaceful march, advertising for magazines, etc.
- A television news report could be written and acted out.
- Plan an 'issues day' where students present their materials to the class.

Journalism: Suffrage newspaper

Explore *The White Ribbon*, the first newspaper run by women in New Zealand, and prepare to make your own.

- Gather information and articles about different suffrage topics.
- Give your newspaper a 'suffrage' name.
- Put it all together, then copy and distribute.

Speech writing: A dramatic presentation

Students prepare a speech on women's suffrage.

- Students will research and prepare their speech and then present it to the class in a dramatic fashion, dressed in vintage clothing.

Write: Poetry

Choose a topic and write a poem on it. Decorate your poem for presentation.

Topics could include: a modern women's issue, women's suffrage, a suffragist or woman you admire, traditional women's roles etc.

Write: Suffragist biography

Choose one of the New Zealand suffragists that appear in the photographs on pages 25–27 or in the 1893 Women's Suffrage Petition online database.

- Teach information literacy, including how to research people.
- Book a women's suffrage themed visit to your local library where the librarian can talk about places to research.
- Use the library's freely available databases such as Ancestry.com (which includes the New Zealand electoral rolls) and Findmypast.
- Search freely available online databases such as Papers Past, FamilySearch and Birth, Death and Marriage Historical Records.

? Suffrage quiz

1. Suffrage is:

   a) the right to vote
   b) the right for women to vote
   c) the women who fought for women's rights
   d) the petitioning for women's rights

2. Circle the three colours of the New Zealand suffrage movement:

   a) pink — unconditional love and understanding
   b) gold — enlightenment and courage
   c) white — purity of purpose
   d) violet — dignity and self-respect

3. Suffragist Kate Sheppard was born on 10 March 1848. When was Eliza born?

   a) 10 March 1948
   b) 30 March 1848
   c) 10 March 1946
   d) 30 March 1846

4. What is a suffragist?

   a) a person who uses law-abiding, non-violent means to gain the vote for women, including petitions, lobbying and marches
   b) a man or woman who believes that women should be given the vote
   c) an individual who supports suffrage
   d) someone who is in favour of women having the right to vote, especially in societies where women are not allowed to vote

5. The introduction of what became a symbol of freedom of movement and independence for women in the 1880s?

   a) Penny Farthing bicycle
   b) Kaimanawa horse
   c) brassiere
   d) modern bicycle

6. What was the flower worn by people supporting women's right to vote in New Zealand:

   a) blue hydrangea
   b) red tulip
   c) white camellia
   c) yellow daffodil

7. What did the Anti-Women's Franchise League give members of Parliament to encourage them to vote against women's suffrage?

   a) red camellias
   b) white feathers
   c) green cufflinks
   d) pink handkerchiefs

8. Who asked the Māori parliament in 1893 to allow Māori women to vote for candidates and serve on it?

   a) Princess Te Puea Hērangi
   b) Meri Te Tai Mangakāhia
   c) Dame Whina Cooper
   d) Kate Sheppard

9. Which was the first self-governing country in the world to grant women the vote?

   a) Massachusetts
   b) Cook Islands
   c) New Zealand
   d) Pitcairn Islands

10. Who was the first woman mayor in the British Empire

    a) Elizabeth Yates — New Zealand
    b) Susanna M. Salter — United States
    c) Catherine Tizard — New Zealand
    d) Elizabeth Garrett Anderson — England

11. In May 1895 the first New Zealand newspaper to be owned and operated solely by women was issued. What was it called?

    a) The Lily
    b) The Revolution
    c) The White Ribbon
    d) Women's Journal

12. Although the first-wave feminists had won the vote in 1893 they were not allowed to stand for Parliament until 1919. What was the year and name of the first woman elected for parliament?

    a) 1893 John Hall
    b) 1933 Elizabeth McCombs
    c) 1983 Sonja Davies
    d) 2017 Jacinda Ardern

13. What New Zealand note commemorates women's suffrage?

    a) $2
    b) $5
    c) $10
    d) $20

14. When was the 100th anniversary of women's suffrage in New Zealand?

    a) 1893
    b) 1993
    c) 2003
    d) 2043

Suffrage quiz answers

1. a) the right to vote
2. b) gold c) white and d) violet
3. d) 30 March 1846
4. all
5. d) modern bicycle
6. c) white camellia
7. a) red camellias
8. b) Meri Te Tai Mangakāhia
9. c) New Zealand
10. a) Elizabeth Yates — New Zealand
11. c) The White Ribbon
12. b) 1933 Elizabeth McCombs
13. c) $10
14. b) 1993

37

Glossary

Baby Farming paid caregivers who may have neglected children in their care, concealed their deaths or deliberately murdered the infants

c. *circa* around or about, when dates not exactly known

Cabinet ministers chosen by the ruling party to run Government

Candidate a person seeking or being considered for some kind of position like being elected to an office (a position of authority or service)

Colony a country or area under the full or partial political control of a more powerful country that is often far away

Colonisation the forming of a settlement or colony by a group of people who seek to take control of a place. It usually involves large-scale immigration of people to a 'new' location and the expansion of their civilisation and culture into this area. Colonisation may involve dominating the original indigenous inhabitants of the area

Democracy literally, 'rule by the people'. A system of government in which power is vested either in the people, who rule directly or through freely elected representatives

Election choosing between people by voting for whom you prefer

Electorate the people in a certain area who are entitled to vote in an election

Emigrate to leave one's country to live permanently in another

Feminists: first-wave (1830s–early 1900s) focus on legal issues throughout the Western world, mainly on gaining the right to vote

Feminists: second-wave (1960s–1980s) post-World War II and including minority group women. Focus on social equality and women's reproductive rights during the anti-war and civil rights movements, including minority group women

Feminists: third-wave (1990s–2000s) post-colonial and post-modern thinking. Focus on equal pay, women's reproductive rights and ending violence against women while embracing the term 'feminism'

Feminists: fourth-wave (2012–present) focus on justice for women, unfair pay and work conditions and gender equality, the small number of women in politics and business and pressures of unrealistic body image. Campaigns in response to violence against women

Franchise the right to vote for Parliament in public elections

Gaol common spelling of jail used between c.1760 and 1830

Gold, White and Violet (Give Women the Vote) the colours used to represent suffrage in New Zealand and the United States. In 1913 purple, white and gold were declared the official colours of the United States National Woman's Party (NWP)

Government the majority party or group of parties in Parliament

Illegitimate born of parents not lawfully married to each other

Immigrate come into another country to live permanently

Indentured an employee who is bound by a signed or forced contract (indenture) to work for a particular employer for a fixed time

Independent an individual politician not affiliated with any political party

Journeyman a skilled worker who has completed an apprenticeship

Larceny theft of personal property

League an organisation formed by a group with a common goal

Legislate when a government or state legislates, it passes a new law

Legislation the laws passed by Parliament, considered collectively

Legislature a group with the authority to make laws for a government

Lobby trying to influence a member of parliament, the term comes from discussions taking place in the lobby of parliament buildings

Master Bricklayer a much respected exceptional craftsman with technical authority and years of experience on the job

Ministers the senior Members of Parliament (MPs) chosen by the Government to look after its business

New Zealand House of Representatives democratically elected group of Members of Parliament (MPs). Passes all laws, provides ministers to form a Cabinet, and supervises the work of the Government

New Zealand Parliament (Pāremata Aotearoa) legislature (group with authority to make laws) includes the House of Representatives and the monarch (usually represented by the governor-general)

Parliament elected members of the House of Representatives in New Zealand

Petition a document signed by many people. Aimed at influencing government of some other authority

Phalanx ancient Greek term, an organised body of people standing or moving in close formation together into battle, in order to destroy the enemy's morale

Prohibition forbidding by law the making or selling of alcohol

Provincial Council local governing bodies of the Provinces of New Zealand (1853-1876)

Representatives Members of Parliament (MPs) representing various districts or electorates

Stamens camellia flowers have a cluster of golden-yellow, prominent stamens in their centre. A stamen is the pollen producing part of a flower

Sovereign supreme ruler, especially a monarch

Suffrage the right to vote, or the campaigning for the right to vote

Suffragist a person using law-abiding, non-violent means to gain the vote, including petitions, lobbying, marches and publicity stunts

Suffragette members of the suffrage movement who resorted to a more militant approach in Britain from 1903. The term dates from 1906 and uses the suffix 'ette' to belittle these women, who soon took up the name with pride. They chained themselves to railings, disrupted public meetings and damaged public property. They were arrested and imprisoned, but continued their protest in prison by hunger strike, which led to brutal force-feeding. In 1913, Emily Davison stepped out in front of the King's horse at the Epsom Derby, was hit, and later died from her injuries. The movement halted in 1914 in order to support the war effort. In 1918, the British Parliament passed legislation permitting some women the vote, but full suffrage was not gained until 1928

Temperance giving up or avoiding the use of alcohol (the 'demon drink')

Taonga treasure, anything prized

Index

Acknowledgements

Many people have helped this book upon its journey, whether a piece of missing information, photographs, being exceptionally helpful or encouraging, or the dreaded proofreading. These include: Andrea Bell (Hocken, University of Otago); Julia Bradshaw (Canterbury Museum); Jennifer Cook (proofreading); Glenn Coster (Christchurch City Libraries); Jared Davidson (Archives New Zealand); Ian Fraser (great grandson of Eliza); Ynys Fraser QSM (née Wallis) (granddaugher of Eliza); Keith Giles (Auckland Libraries; Denise Grant (Invercargill City Libraries & Archives); Penny Guy (proofreading); Shannon Hall-McLachlan (Linwood Cemetery historian); Lynley Hood (researcher & author); Megan Jones (editing); Fiona Kean (proofreading); Kathryn (Kate) Kersey (Bearsted & Thurnham historian & author); Stefanie Lash (Archives New Zealand); Jamie Mackay (Ministry for Culture and NZ History); Frances Moss (great-granddaughter of Eliza); Helen Smith (Alexander Turnbull Library); Gábor Tóth (Wellington City Libraries); Barbara Turner (proofreading).

MAUAO PUBLISHING
AOTEAROA NEW ZEALAND

Published by Mauao Publishing
101 Hynds Road, Gate Pā, Tauranga 3112
AOTEAROA NEW ZEALAND
www.facebook.com/mauaopublishing

Copyright © Debbie McCauley, 2018

First Published 28 November 2018

ISBN: 978-0-473-44946-9

Author: Debbie McCauley
Illustrator: Helen Casey
Translator: Tamati Waaka
Design and layout: Sarah Elworthy

Printed in China by Asia Pacific Offset (Hong Kong)

A catalogue record for this book is available from the National Library of New Zealand (Kei te pātengi raraunga o Te Puna Mātauranga o Aotearoa te whakarārangi o tēnei pukapuka.

Picture credits

Endpapers: various suffrage cartoons from the 1890s. Page 2: Map reproduced courtesy of the Kent Archaeological Society. Page 4: Backyards of houses in Tory Street, Wellington (Wilkinson Sword Group NZ: Photographs of the Bryant and May, Bell and Co Ltd factory in Tory Street, Wellington. Ref: 1/1-026013-G. Alexander Turnbull Library, Wellington, NZ / records/22590952); Public meeting (Wellington independent. Ref: Eph-C-POLITICS-1853-03. Alexander Turnbull Library, Wellington, NZ/ records/23133176); Voting Paper: Published in 'Miscellaneous bills and documents relating to the Wellington Provincial Council elections of 1853' (Ref: B-K-63-001, Col: Pq 993.1 WEL 1853, Alexander Turnbull Library, Wellington, NZ). Page 5: New Zealand Company Coat of Arms (Archives New Zealand: NZC34 Box 12/ 17). Page 6: Bricklayer (iStock Stock illustration ID:182227632); Dinner on board the first emigrant ship for New Zealand (Auckland, Star Lithographic Works, 1890. Ref: A-109-054. Alexander Turnbull Library, Wellington, New Zealand. /records/22355844); Ware Street brickfield remains (Kathryn Kersey). Page 7: Arrival of the Tyne (1841) (National Library of New Zealand Te Puna Mātauranga o Aotearoa: New Zealand Gazette and Wellington Spectator, 14 August 1841, p. 1); Port Nicholson (Heaphy, Charles, 1820-1881: Port Nicholson, New Zealand; comprehending about one third of the water frontage of the town of Wellington, April, 1841. T. Allom lith. London, Published for the New Zealand Company by Smith Elder & Co. printed by C. Hullmandel [1842]. Ref: C-026-001-b. Alexander Turnbull Library, Wellington, New Zealand. /records/22344237). Page 8: Convict irons (iStock); Handcoloured woodcut of the dockyard under construction on the Ireland Island Bermuda showing four prison hulks. The hill towards the left was levelled by quarrying (Illustrated London News, 29 July 1848); View near Woolwich in Kent showing the employment of the convicts from the hulks, c.1800 (LRHS: 'London: Printed for Bowles & Carver' LLHS: 'No. 69 St Paul's Church Yard'. State Library of New South Wales FL3233506). Page 9: New Zealand Company Advertisement, 1839 (http://deacademic.com/pictures/dewiki/78/New_Zealand_Company_Advert.jpg); Punch:Here and there or, emigration a remedy. London, 8 July 1848 (Ref: PUBL-0043-1848-15. Alexander Turnbull Library, Wellington, New Zealand. /records/23241802). Page 10: Crowd outside the tobbaconist shop of R Farmer, on the corner of Perry and Queen Streets, Masterton (Ref: 1/2-011707. Alexander Turnbull Library, Wellington, New Zealand. /records/23160926); Eliza Hart and John Wallis wedding certificate 1863 (Frances Moss); John Wallis (Frances Moss); Purification. New Zealand Graphic, 18 November 1893 p. 417 (Sir George Grey Special Collections, Auckland Libraries, NZG-18931118-417-1). Page 12: Temperance demonstration in Pitt Street, Auckland on Election day, 25 November 1902 (Sir George Grey Special Collections, Auckland Libraries, AWNS-19021204-1-2); What, dinner not ready yet! What have you been doing? (a cartoon by William Blomfield 1866-1938. Ref: 1/2-031495-F. Alexander Turnbull Library, Wellington, New Zealand. /records/23251788). Page 13: Eliza Townsend (née Wallis), 1910 (Frances Moss); Notice to epicene women. Electioneering women are requested not to call here (Wright, Henry Charles Clarke, 1844-1936: 12706 - Alex Ferguson, Printer, Wellington. [1902]. Ref: Eph-B-WOMEN-1902-01. Alexander Turnbull Library, Wellington, New Zealand. /records/22872683). Page 14: Esther Wallis Dean and the rest of the children taken after their arrest from the Deans' home in East Winton, known as The Larches, 1895 (Invercargill City Library). Page 15: Children at Saint Saviour's Orphanage, Christchurch (Ref: 1/1-007229-G. Alexander Turnbull Library, Wellington, New Zealand. /records/22590898). Page 16: Maori Dress Reformers (Christchurch City Libraries, The weekly press, 14 Feb. 1906, p. 42, File reference: CCL-PhotoCD11-IMG0096); Young Maori woman in a rational dress outfit with her bicycle (New Zealand Graphic, 11 May 1895, p. 438, Sir George Grey Special Collections, Auckland Libraries, NZG-18950511-438-1). Page 17: The New Zealand Suffrage Centennial Medal 1993 (New Zealand Defence Force). Page 18: Digitising the 1893 women's suffrage petition (Photograph by Mark Beatty, Archives New Zealand Te Rua Mahara o te Kāwanatanga); The 1893 Women's Suffrage Petition (Archives New Zealand Te Rua Mahara o te Kāwanatanga); The 1893 Women's Suffrage Petition in 1985 just before restoration work was started (ARCH 458 1 am 1 1984, http://www.famnet.net.nz/newsletters/famnet/April_2012/April_2012.htm); The 'Carpet Knight', Sir John Hall covers the floor of the House with a little petition (New Zealand Graphic 12 August 1893 p. 84 Sir George Grey Special Collections, Auckland Libraries, 7-A12355). Page 19: First issue of The White Ribbon, May 1895 (Tauranga City Libraries, microfilm). Page 20: Election Day, New Plymouth, 1893 (George Herbert White PHO2008-626, collection of Puke Ariki, New Plymouth); Election Day, New Plymouth, 1893 (George Herbert White PHO2008-633, collection of Puke Ariki, New Plymouth); photograph of an engraving showing women going to the poll at Devonport, 1893 (Ref: MNZ-2834-1/4-F. Alexander Turnbull Library, Wellington, New Zealand./records/22630436); Women vote at their first election, Tahakopa (McWhannell, Rhoda Leslie (Mrs), 1898-1996: Photographs of forestry and farming at Ohaupo. Ref: PA1-0-550-34-1. Alexander Turnbull Library, Wellington, New Zealand./records/22311886); Victory Women's Franchise Passed, September 8th, 1893 (New Zealand Graphic 16 September 1893, Sir George Grey Special Collections, Auckland Libraries, NZG-18930916-201-1). Page 21: National Library of New Zealand Te Puna Mātauranga o Aotearoa: Daily Telegraph (19 September 1893, p. 3); National Library of New Zealand Te Puna Mātauranga o Aotearoa: Star (21 September 1893, p. 3); National Library of New Zealand Te Puna Mātauranga o Aotearoa: New Zealand Times (28 November 1893, p. 2). Page 22: Camellia 'Kate Sheppard' (The Plant Store, 2018); Grave of Eliza and John Wallis at Linwood Cemetery (Photo: Shannon Hall-McLachlan, Friends of Linwood Cemetery Charitable Trust); postcard from Kate Sheppard to Eliza Wallis, 1903 (Moss collection, CCL-FrMo-KS-PC-1, Frances Moss & Christchurch City Libraries); postcard from Kate Sheppard to Eliza Wallis, 1903 (Moss collection, CCL-FrMo-KS-PC-2, Frances Moss & Christchurch City Libraries); Women approach the polling booth at the Drill Hall in Rutland Street, Auckland, during the General Election on 6 December 1899 (Sir George Grey Special Collections, Auckland Libraries, 7-A12353). Page 23: New Zealanders taking part in a suffragette procession to Hyde Park, London, with 15,000 people, 23 July 1910 (Supplement to the Auckland Weekly News, 8 September 1910, Sir George Grey Special Collections, Auckland Libraries, AWNS-19100908-9-2); The order of the red camellia (Evening Post, 16 September 1893 p. 3, National Library of New Zealand Te Puna Mātauranga o Aotearoa). Page 24: 1892 Suffrage Petition – Sheet 234, No. 418 & 419 (Archives New Zealand Te Rua Mahara o te Kāwanatanga); 1893 Suffrage Petition – Sheets 1 & 532 (Archives New Zealand Te Rua Mahara o te Kāwanatanga). Page 25: The convention called by the Canterbury Women's Institute which resulted in the formation of the National Council of the Women of New Zealand, 1896. The convenors and the delegates are shown outside the Provincial Council Chambers (Christchurch City Libraries. File reference: CCL-PhotoCD08-IMG0086); The Women's Council (Published 23 April 1896, p. 26, Canterbury Times, Bishop collection, Canterbury Museum. Ref: 1923.53.802). Page 26: The National Council of Women held at Christchurch, April 1896 (Artist Unknown, Supplement to The Otago Daily Times October 17, 1896. Hocken Collections, Uare Taoka o Hākena, University of Otago). Page 27: Suratura Tea – Nature's product, not blended with Indian or China teas (Wm Gregg & Co. Agents for Otago, 1896, lithograph: 422 x 562mm; on paper: 502 x 632mm, 15,892, Hocken Collections, Uare Taoka o Hākena, University of Otago). Page 28: Eliza and John Wallis' house at 49 Ensors Road, Christchurch (Frances Moss); The Sweating System (Blomfield, William, 1866-1938: New Zealand Observer and Free Lance, 3 November 1888. Ref: H-713-093. Alexander Turnbull Library, Wellington, New Zealand. /records/22331016). Page 32: Catherine Tizard, 16th Governor-General New Zealand (Government House); Helen Clark, 37th Prime Minister of New Zealand (2007-02-16 02:42 Jughead78 2300×2780×8 (1291083 bytes) this photo has been granted a GFDL lisence by the owner: "the office of the prime minister" www. primeminister.govt.nz contact: Antony Rhodes. Wikimedia Commons); Iriaka Rātana, first female Māori MP (head and shoulders portrait of Iriaka Matiu Rātana. Photograph taken c. 1949. Tesla Studio. Wikimedia Commons); Jacinda Ardern, 40th Prime Minister of New Zealand (cropped image of Jacinda Ardern at the swearing-in ceremony on the 26th of October 2017. Governor-General New Zealand. Wikimedia Commons); Jenny Shipley, 36th Prime Minister of New Zealand (Dame Jenny Shipley, 36th Prime Minister of New Zealand, attending the Wellington celebration hosted by the Minister of Women's Affairs, Hon Jo Goodhew at Parliament on the anniversary of suffrage day, 19 September. New Zealand Ministry for Women. Wikimedia Commons); Mabel Howard (Labour Member of Parliament Mabel Howard had strong ties with the working-class Sydenham electorate, which she represented from 1946 to 1969. She was an advocate for consumers, and is often remembered for waving two differing 'OS' (oversize or extra large) pairs of women's bloomers in Parliament in 1954. Her aim was to show the importance of having standard clothing sizes. Dominion Post photographer. Wikimedia Commons). Page 34: Knitted suffragist camellia; Paper plate suffragist camellia; little sewn suffragist rosette (all Maia McCauley); make a suffragist hat (Debbie McCauley). Page 35: Paper suffragist sash (Debbie McCauley).

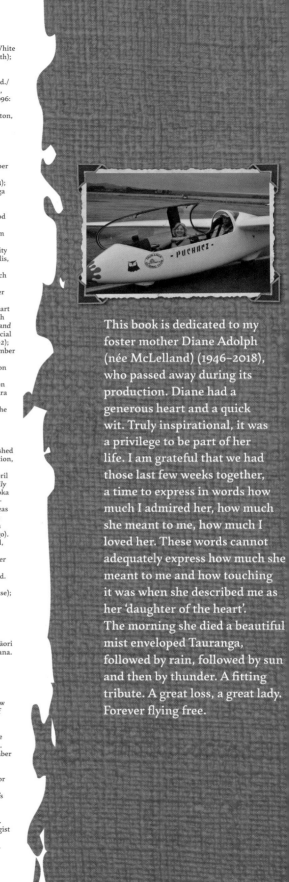

This book is dedicated to my foster mother Diane Adolph (née McLelland) (1946–2018), who passed away during its production. Diane had a generous heart and a quick wit. Truly inspirational, it was a privilege to be part of her life. I am grateful that we had those last few weeks together, a time to express in words how much I admired her, how much she meant to me, how much I loved her. These words cannot adequately express how much she meant to me and how touching it was when she described me as her 'daughter of the heart'. The morning she died a beautiful mist enveloped Tauranga, followed by rain, followed by sun and then by thunder. A fitting tribute. A great loss, a great lady. Forever flying free.